Ice Cream and Sorbets

Abbreviations and units of measurement:

CH = carbohydrate

cl   = centilitre (1 cl is equal to 10 ml)

F   = fat

g   = gram

kg = kilogram

ml = millilitre

l   = litre

P   = protein

tbsp = tablespoon

tsp = teaspoon

FDM = fat in dry matter

The recipes in this book are made without an ice cream maker.
Many of them can, however, be made using an ice cream maker
and these recipes are specially marked in the Index. Please check
your ice cream maker's capacity and adjust the quantities where
necessary.

Ice Cream and Sorbets

Contents

Introduction

Delicious ice cream creations

Fancy an ice cream? Then save yourself the trip to the ice cream parlour or the supermarket and simply make your favourite ice cream yourself. It is as easy as pie with the tempting recipes in this book. Be it creamy milk, cream or fruit ice cream, light sorbets and granitas, melt-in-your-mouth parfaits or fresh ideas with yoghurt – you will find your favourites here! The Gelateria features sophisticated recipes for popular ice cream parlour classics such as spaghetti ice cream, caramel ice cream, tartufo or iced coffee.

Ice cream specialities

The range of irresistible frozen delights from the ice cream maker or the freezer extends from popular ice cream specialities like milk, cream or fruit ice cream through to melting parfaits as well as refreshing granitas and sorbets.

Ice cream

Milk- and/or cream-based ice cream is essentially a combination of milk and/or cream, eggs, sugar and various flavourings such as chocolate, nuts, alcohol, fruit purées or fruit juices (fruit ice cream has a fruit content of at least 20%). The ice cream mixture needs to be stirred regularly with a fork during freezing in order to prevent ice crystals from forming – this takes place automatically in an ice cream maker.

Parfaits

A parfait is mainly comprised of egg yolk which has been beaten with sugar over a bain-marie until thick and creamy. Whipped cream, whisked egg whites and flavouring ingredients can then be added. The addition of cream and whisked egg whites gives it a lighter consistency and allows only small ice crystals to form. Unlike ice cream, parfaits are not stirred during their preparation (e.g. in an ice cream maker). Instead, the mixture is left in the freezer to freeze.

Sorbets

Sorbets are made from sugar syrups flavoured with fruit purée, fruit juice or tea, sometimes with alcohol (such as Champagne). As a rule, sorbets include neither milk products nor eggs – whisked egg whites at most, to make them fluffier and lighter. Sorbets need to be stirred several times during freezing to produce a smooth, creamy mixture.

Granitas

In contrast to sorbets, granitas – a combination of a drink and an ice lolly – are not mixed through during freezing. Instead, the surface layer of ice is repeatedly broken into rough pieces with a wooden spoon to produce grainy ice crystals. This is also why granitas cannot be made in a conventional ice cream maker.

Tips & Tricks

- When making ice cream and sorbet, stir the mixture regularly with a fork during freezing to keep the mixture smooth and to prevent ice crystals from forming.

- Take the ice cream out of the freezer several minutes before serving so that it can thaw slightly. This makes it easier to shape and it tastes creamier and more intense.

- If you are using an ice cream maker do be sure to check the machine's capacity and, in general, prepare smaller quantities each time so that the ice cream really freezes properly.

- Use finely granulated sugar or caster sugar for making ice cream; large-grained sugar does not dissolve as well.

- Note that the addition of alcohol extends the freezing time and makes the ice cream softer. The same applies to the addition of fat.

Refreshing granitas

Melon granita
with mint

Serves 4

400 g watermelon

½ bunch mint

½ lime

mint leaves for garnishing

Preparation time: 15 minutes
 (plus freezing time)
Per serving approx.
 54 kcal/226 kJ
1 g P, 1 g F, 9 g CH

1 Peel and de-seed the watermelon, and then chop the flesh into small pieces. Wash the mint, shake dry and remove 10 leaves. Squeeze the juice from the lime.

2 Purée the watermelon pieces together with the lime juice and the mint leaves in a food processor. Freeze the mixture, stirring it frequently with a fork. Divide the granita between four glasses and serve garnished with mint leaves.

Blood orange granita
with honey

Serves 4

6–8 blood oranges
1 untreated orange
150 g blossom honey

Preparation time: 15 minutes
  (plus freezing time)
Per serving approx.
  255 kcal/1068 kJ
3 g P, 1 g F, 56 g CH

1 Squeeze the juice from the blood oranges and measure out 400 ml. Wash the untreated orange under warm water, dry and grate the zest.

2 Purée the juice, zest and honey in a food processor, and place in the freezer to freeze. Stir it through frequently during freezing. Divide the granita between the glasses and serve immediately.

Strawberry granita
lovely and light

Serves 4

125 g icing sugar
500 g strawberries
2 tbsp lemon juice

Preparation time: 20 minutes
 (plus cooling and freezing
 time)
Per serving approx.
 124 kcal/519 kJ
1 g P, 1 g F, 27 g CH

1 Pour the sugar into a saucepan together with 125 ml of water and stir until dissolved, bring to the boil and simmer for 5 minutes. Leave to cool. Wash the strawberries and then purée them in a food processor together with the lemon juice. Stir in the sugar syrup.

2 Strain the strawberry purée through a sieve into a bowl and freeze for approx. 6 hours, stirring it frequently with a fork during freezing. Divide between the glasses and serve immediately.

TIP

Fresh strawberries are widely available from markets and supermarkets. Ideally, this healthy fruit should be enjoyed or processed right after purchasing as it is highly susceptible to bruising and perishes quickly.

Cranberry granita
with limoncello and vodka

Serves 4

50 ml limoncello

50 ml vodka

5 tbsp lime juice

8 tbsp cranberry juice

3 tbsp sugar

slices of fruit for
  garnishing

Preparation time: 30 minutes
  (plus cooling and freezing
  time)

Per serving approx.
  222 kcal/929 kJ

4 g P, 1 g F, 49 g CH

1 Combine the limoncello, vodka, lime juice and
cranberry juice. Add the sugar to 100 ml of water
and stir over a medium heat until dissolved. Stir in the
other ingredients and leave to cool.

2 Pour the mixture into a shallow bowl and leave to
freeze in the freezer for approx. 5 hours. Stir frequently during this time to fold in the ice crystals.

3 Allow the granita to thaw slightly before serving
and then transfer to glasses, garnish with fruit
slices and serve immediately.

Citrus granita
with honey

Serves 4

1 untreated orange
1 untreated grapefruit
1 untreated lime
1 untreated lemon
200 ml mineral water
50 g blossom honey
4 lemon balm leaves

Preparation time: 15 minutes
  (plus cooling and freezing
  time)
Per serving approx.
  121 kcal/507 kJ
1 g P, 1 g F, 22 g CH

1 Wash and dry all of the fruit, and peel the zest into very thin strips. Squeeze the juice from the fruit and strain. Bring the mineral water to the boil with the honey and leave to cool.

2 Combine the fruit juice with the finely chopped zest and the chopped lemon balm; stir into the honey syrup. Pour into a bowl and freeze.

3 Stir with a fork several times. Divide among glasses and serve immediately.

Hibiscus flower granita
with honey

Serves 4

2 tbsp sugar

5 tsp dried hibiscus flowers

2 tbsp pear syrup

3 tbsp acacia honey

1 tsp lemon juice

untreated hibiscus flowers
  for garnishing

Preparation time: 20 minutes
  (plus freezing time)
Per serving approx.
  51 kcal/214 kJ
1 g P, 1 g F, 12 g CH

1 Add the sugar to 500 ml of water and bring to the boil. Add the hibiscus flowers, bring to the boil, cover and leave to infuse for 10 minutes. Strain the mixture through a sieve. Combine the hibiscus tea with the pear syrup, the acacia honey and the lemon juice.

2 Pour the mixture into a shallow bowl and freeze for approx. 5 hours, stirring frequently during that time so that the granita will be nice and grainy. Divide among dessert bowls and garnish with hibiscus flowers before serving.

Grapefruit granita

wonderfully refreshing

Serves 4
250 g sugar
350 ml grapefruit juice
60 ml blood orange juice

Preparation time: 20 minutes
(plus cooling and freezing
time)
Per serving approx.
513 kcal/2148 kJ
1 g P, 1 g F, 126 g CH

1 Dissolve the sugar in 800 ml of water in a saucepan, stirring all the time, and then leave to cool. Mix the grapefruit juice and blood orange juice with the cooled sugar syrup.

2 Freeze the granita for approx. 4 hours, stirring it several times. Distribute among glasses and serve immediately.

TIP

Grapefruits are a hybrid of pomelos and oranges. They can be categorised into the white-fleshed, mostly European varieties, the milder, pink-fleshed varieties and the sweet, red-fleshed varieties. A medium-sized grapefruit provides the whole of the daily vitamin C requirement and also contains vitamins A, B1, B2, B6, niacin and folic acid, as well as minerals.

Yoghurt honey granita
with sesame brittle

Serves 4

80 g blossom honey

400 g yoghurt

1 untreated lemon

2 tbsp sugar

1½ tbsp sesame seeds

1 tsp butter

2 tbsp raspberry syrup

Preparation time: 15 minutes
  (plus freezing, caramelising
  and cooling time)
Per serving approx.
  181 kcal/758 kJ
4 g P, 6 g F, 27 g CH

1 Mix together the honey and the yoghurt. Wash the lemon in warm water, dry and cut in half. Put one half aside to use in another recipe. Grate the zest of the other half, squeeze out the juice and then stir the zest and the juice into the honey-yoghurt mixture. Freeze for approx. 5 hours, stirring several times.

2 In the meantime, caramelise the sugar in a frying pan. Stir in the sesame seeds and the butter, spread over a sheet of baking paper and leave to cool. Break the sesame brittle into pieces as soon as it is hard.

3 Transfer the granita into glasses, drizzle with the raspberry syrup and garnish with the sesame brittle.

Espresso granita
with cream

Serves 4

350 ml espresso
4 tsp sugar syrup
12 ice cubes
2 tbsp whipped cream
cocoa powder for dusting

Preparation time: 15 minutes
   (plus freezing time)
Per serving approx.
   34 kcal/142 kJ
1 g P, 1 g F, 5 g CH

1 Leave the espresso to cool then mix with the sugar syrup. Crush the ice cubes and place half of the quantity in the cups.

2 Purée the rest of the crushed ice cubes with the espresso and sugar syrup. Gradually fold in the cream. Place the espresso granita in the cups and serve. Dust with cocoa powder if desired.

Pomegranate granita
with grape juice

Serves 4

5 pomegranates

6 tbsp pomegranate
  syrup

5 tbsp sugar

500 ml red grape juice

2 limes

1 untreated lemon

Preparation time: 25 minutes
  (plus cooling and freezing
  time)

Per serving approx.
  293 kcal/1227 kJ

2 g P, 3 g F, 58 g CH

1 Cut the pomegranates in half and scoop out the seeds. Place the seeds in a saucepan and combine with the pomegranate syrup and the sugar. Pour in 150 ml of the grape juice and simmer for approx. 5 minutes. Purée briefly in a food processor, then strain and leave to cool.

2 Wash and dry the limes and then squeeze out their juice. Mix the lime juice together with the rest of the grape juice and stir into the pomegranate mixture. Freeze for approx. 5 hours, stirring from the outside inwards several times.

3 Wash and dry the lemon and cut into slices. Transfer the granita to glasses and garnish with lemon slices before serving.

Coconut almond granita
exotic sophistication

Serves 4

200 ml almond milk

100 ml coconut milk

2 tbsp sugar

75 g fresh coconut flesh

25 g chopped almonds

Preparation time: 15 minutes
  (plus freezing time)
Per serving approx.
  253 kcal/1059 kJ
5 g P, 19 g F, 13 g CH

1 Combine the almond milk with the coconut milk and dissolve the sugar in the mixture. Finely chop the fresh coconut flesh and add to the milk mixture together with the chopped almonds.

2 Freeze the mixture for approx. 4 hours, stirring with a fork several times. Purée the granita in a food processor if you prefer and divide among glasses. Serve immediately.

TIP

Coconuts are the fruit of the tropical coconut palm. Coconut milk is made by pressing the flesh of the coconut – not to be confused with the coconut water found inside the coconut.

Sophisticated sorbets

Orange sorbet
with Campari

Serves 4

75 ml Campari

400 ml freshly squeezed
  orange juice

60 g sugar

2 egg whites

80 g icing sugar

candied orange peel for
  decorating

Preparation time: 25 minutes
  (plus cooling and freezing
  time)

Per serving approx.
  154 kcal/645 kJ

3 g P, 1 g F, 33 g CH

1 Combine the Campari with 375 ml of the orange juice and the sugar, stirring until the sugar has dissolved. Place the mixture in the freezer for 2 hours.

2 Beat the egg whites together with the icing sugar and the rest of the orange juice until stiff. Fold into the orange-Campari mixture, place in a shallow bowl and leave in the freezer for approx. 6 hours, stirring thoroughly every hour.

3 Use an ice cream scoop to divide the sorbet between the glasses or simply squeeze the sorbet through a piping bag. Sprinkle with candied orange peel and serve.

Sparkling wine sorbet
with mango and strawberries

Serves 4

1 untreated lemon
1 vanilla pod
500 ml sparkling wine
150 g sugar
1 mango
200 g strawberries

Preparation time: 20 minutes
   (plus cooling and freezing
   time)
Per serving approx.
   215 kcal/900 kJ
1 g P, 1 g F, 47 g CH

1 Wash the lemon in warm water and rub dry. Grate approx. 1 teaspoon of zest. Cut the vanilla pod open lengthways and scrape out the seeds. Mix the sparkling wine together with the sugar, heat in a saucepan and stir until the sugar has dissolved. Add the vanilla pod, the vanilla seeds and the lemon zest, and leave to cool.

2 Remove the vanilla pod. Pour the mixture into a shallow bowl and place in the freezer to freeze for approx. 5 hours, stirring several times.

3 Peel the mango and cut the flesh from the stone in strips. Wash the strawberries, pat dry and cut in half. Arrange the fruit on plates together with scoops of the sparkling wine sorbet and serve.

Papaya sorbet
fruity and fresh

Serves 4

2 papayas (200 g each)
2 tbsp lemon juice
1 vanilla pod
150 g icing sugar
1 egg white
salt

Preparation time: 20 minutes
  (plus cooling, cooking and
  freezing time)
Per serving approx.
  90 kcal/396 kJ
1 g P, 1 g F, 18 g CH

1 Cut the papayas in half, remove the pips, scoop out the flesh and cut into cubes. Combine with the lemon juice and purée in a food processor. Cover and chill.

2 Cut the vanilla pod in half. Scrape out the seeds and place both the pod and the seeds in a saucepan together with the icing sugar and 250 ml of water. Bring to the boil, stirring all the time until the sugar has dissolved. Leave to cool then remove the vanilla pod.

3 Combine the sugar syrup with the papaya purée and leave in the freezer to freeze for approx. 5 hours, stirring thoroughly several times. Beat the egg white together with a pinch of salt until stiff and fold into the sorbet. Leave to freeze again.

Pineapple sorbet
with lime

Serves 4

850 ml pineapple juice,
  unsweetened

350 g sugar

3 tbsp lime juice

1 egg white

salt

Preparation time: 25 minutes
  (plus cooking, cooling and
  freezing time)

Per serving approx.
  488 kcal/2043 kJ

2 g P, 1 g F, 116 g CH

1 Stir together the juice and the sugar in a saucepan until the sugar has dissolved. Bring to the boil and simmer for approx. 5 minutes. Leave to cool then stir in the lime juice. Pour into a metal bowl and leave to freeze for approx. 5 hours, stirring thoroughly with a fork several times to avoid formation of ice crystals.

2 Beat the egg white together with a pinch of salt until stiff then fold into the sorbet, to produce a smooth mixture. Leave to harden in the freezer. Distribute among glasses and serve.

TIP

For egg white to beat stiffly the eggs need to be separated carefully so that there is no trace of egg yolk in the egg white. Fat residues in the bowl or on the whisk(s) also prevent beaten egg whites from becoming really stiff. The beaten egg white is stiff when it sticks to the bottom of the upturned bowl or when a cut through it with a knife remains clearly visible. If you beat it for too long the egg white starts to break down and can even revert to its clear state.

Green tea sorbet
with limoncello

Serves 4

2 tbsp green tea leaves

75 g sugar

2 tsp lime juice

4 tbsp limoncello

zest from 1 untreated
  lemon for garnishing

Preparation time: 20 minutes
  (plus infusing, cooling and
  freezing time)
Per serving approx.
  86 kcal/360 kJ
1 g P, 1 g F, 20 g CH

1 Pour 200 ml of boiling water over the tea leaves and leave to draw for one minute. Strain and discard this first infusion. Pour another 400 ml of boiling water over the tea leaves and leave to draw for approx. 4 minutes.

2 Strain the tea into a deep-sided vessel, stir in the sugar and the lime juice, and leave to cool.

3 Pour the mixture into a shallow bowl and place in the freezer for approx. 6 hours, stirring thoroughly every hour. Use an ice cream scoop to transfer to dessert bowls. Drizzle each serving with 1 tablespoon of limoncello and garnish with the lemon zest.

Blackcurrant sorbet
wonderfully fruity

Serves 4

500 g blackcurrants

120 g icing sugar

1 lemon

1 egg white

salt

mint for garnishing

Preparation time: 20 minutes
(plus cooking, cooling and
freezing time)
Per serving approx.
157 kcal/657 kJ
3 g P, 1 g F, 31 g CH

1 Wash the blackcurrants and remove the berries from the stalks. Add the sugar to 120 ml of water in a saucepan, stir until the sugar has dissolved then simmer until it becomes syrupy. Leave to cool.

2 Squeeze the juice from the lemon. Add the juice to the blackcurrants, purée these and then stir in the sugar syrup. Press the mixture through a sieve into a bowl and freeze for approx. 5 hours. Stir well with a fork several times during freezing.

3 Purée the sorbet in a food processor until smooth. Beat the egg white with a pinch of salt until stiff then fold into the sorbet. Return to the freezer to harden. Use an ice cream scoop to transfer the portions into bowls, garnish with mint and serve.

TIP

Blackcurrants and redcurrants are related to the gooseberry, with redcurrants being the most common, but there are also white currants. Blackcurrants are used to make the renowned French liqueur cassis.

Strawberry sorbet
wonderfully refreshing

Serves 4
500 g strawberries
125 g sugar
1 lemon
30 g vanilla sugar

Preparation time: 20 minutes
  (plus infusing, cooking,
  cooling and freezing time)
Per serving approx.
  186 kcal/779 kJ
1 g P, 1 g F, 41 g CH

1 Wash the strawberries and leave to drip dry. Cut them into small pieces and drizzle with the freshly squeezed lemon juice. Leave to draw for 10 minutes.

2 Place 200 ml of water in a saucepan together with the sugar and the vanilla sugar, stirring until the sugar has dissolved, then simmer until syrupy. Leave to cool. Purée the strawberries in a food processor and fold into the syrup.

3 Place the mixture in a bowl and leave in the freezer for approx. 3 hours. Stir through again thoroughly and freeze for a further 3 hours. Place scoops of the sorbet in small bowls to serve.

TIP

In botanical terms strawberries are not berries but an aggregate fruit. They have a very high vitamin C content. Strawberries do not continue ripening once picked and so they should only be bought when in season and ripe.

Blackcurrant tamarillo sorbet
sharply refreshing

Serves 4

100 g sugar

½ clove

grated zest from ¼ of an
  untreated orange

3 tamarillos

200 g blackcurrants, ready
  to use

juice of 1 lemon and
  1 orange

750 ml extra dry sparkling
  wine, champagne or fruit
  juice of your choice

Preparation time: 25 minutes
  (plus cooling and freezing
  time)
Per serving approx.
  230 kcal/963 kJ
2 g P, 1 g F, 44 g CH

1 Place the sugar in a saucepan together with 3 table-spoons of water, the clove and the orange zest, stirring all the time until the sugar has dissolved. Bring to the boil. Strain then leave to cool.

2 Cut the tamarillos in half and scoop out the flesh with a spoon. Purée the blackcurrants together with the tamarillo flesh and the two citrus juices. Press the purée through a sieve and combine with the sugar syrup.

3 Place the sorbet in a shallow bowl in the freezer for 5–6 hours. Take out of the freezer, leave to thaw for approx. 15 minutes and scoop out the portions with an ice cream scoop. Place in dessert bowls or glasses and top up with sparkling wine, champagne or fruit juice as desired.

TIP

Blackcurrants are full of flavour and are also tremendously healthy! They are rich in vitamin C, potassium, iron and numerous trace elements, while their high pectin content helps with digestion problems. Depending on the variety, they contain as little as 40–50 calories per 100 g.

Lemon sorbet
with basil

Serves 4

125 g sugar
3 untreated lemons
4 basil leaves
1 egg white
salt

Preparation time: 20 minutes
(plus cooking, cooling and
freezing time)
Per serving approx.
168 kcal/703 kJ
2 g P, 1 g F, 37 g CH

1 Place the sugar in a saucepan with 250 ml of water. Wash one of the lemons under warm water and peel it. Add the peel to the sugar and stir until the sugar has dissolved. Bring to the boil and simmer for approx. 5 minutes. Leave to cool.

2 Remove the lemon peel. Squeeze the juice from the other two lemons and stir the juice into the sugar syrup. Wash the basil leaves, shake dry, chop finely and stir into the mixture.

3 Freeze the mixture for approx. 5 hours, stir through thoroughly several times. Beat the egg white with a pinch of salt until stiff, fold into the sorbet and stir until smooth. Leave to harden in the freezer. Serve garnished with lemon zest.

Apple sorbet
refreshingly fruity

Serves 4

3 apples
1 tbsp lemon juice
75 g sugar
500 ml apple juice
apple slices for garnishing

Preparation time: 20 minutes
  (plus cooling and freezing
  time)
Per serving approx.
  203 kcal/850 kJ
1 g P, 1 g F, 33 g CH

1 Peel the apples, remove the cores, then purée. Drizzle with the lemon juice. Place the sugar in a saucepan together with 150 ml of water. Stir until the sugar has dissolved, bring to the boil and simmer for approx. 5 minutes until syrupy. Leave to cool.

2 Stir the apple purée into the sugar syrup and place in a bowl. Leave in the freezer for approx. 5 hours, remembering to stir through thoroughly several times.

3 Pour the apple juice into four dessert bowls. Place the sorbet in a piping bag and pipe into the bowls. Serve garnished with apple slices.

Peach sorbet
with Crémant

Serves 4

1 peach

1 tsp sugar

150 ml Crémant

70 g peach sorbet

grated chocolate for
  garnishing

Preparation time: 15 minutes
Per serving approx.
  71 kcal/297 kJ
1 g P, 1 g F, 11 g CH

1 Peel the peach, dice the flesh and combine with the sugar. Divide among four glasses.

2 Whizz half of the Crémant together with the peach sorbet in food processor until smooth. Fold in the rest of the Crémant. Pour over the peach pieces, decorate with grated chocolate as desired and serve immediately.

TIP

You can make the peach sorbet yourself using the recipe for papaya sorbet (see p. 41).

Mint sorbet
wonderfully aromatic

Serves 4
150 g sugar
2 bunches mint
juice of ½ a lemon

Preparation time: 20 minutes
(plus cooling, infusing and
freezing time)
Per serving approx.
162 kcal/678 kJ
1 g P, 1 g F, 39 g CH

1 Place the sugar in a saucepan with 400 ml of water and stir until dissolved. Bring to the boil and leave to cool. Wash the mint, shake dry and pluck the leaves from the stems.

2 Place enough leaves in the sugar syrup to just cover the surface. Leave the mixture to stand for 24 hours, then strain and stir in the lemon juice.

3 Place the liquid in the freezer for 4–5 hours, stirring through several times. Scoop out and serve in small bowls.

Black tea sorbet
with honey

Serves 4

100 g sugar

vanilla pod

2 tbsp black tea leaves

50 g acacia honey

Preparation time: 20 minutes
(plus cooking, cooling and
freezing time)

Per serving approx.
140 kcal/586 kJ
1 g P, 1 g F, 35 g CH

1 Place the sugar in a saucepan with 400 ml of water and stir until dissolved. Bring to the boil. Slice open the vanilla pod and scrape out the seeds. Add the vanilla pod, the vanilla seeds, the tea leaves and the honey to the sugar syrup. Remove the saucepan from the heat and leave to draw for approx. 5 minutes. Strain and leave to cool.

2 Place the liquid in a shallow container and leave in the freezer for approx. 5 hours, stirring through thoroughly several times with a fork.

3 Allow the sorbet to thaw slightly before serving then place in a piping bag. Pipe into dessert bowls or glasses, garnish as desired and serve.

Melon sorbet
with honeydew melon

Serves 4
250 g honeydew melon
125 g sugar
2 tbsp lime juice
1 egg white
salt

Preparation time: 20 minutes
(plus cooking, cooling and
freezing time)
Per serving approx.
175 kcal/733 kJ
1 g P, 1 g F, 37 g CH

1 Peel the melons, remove the pips and dice the flesh. Cover and leave in the freezer.

2 Place the sugar in a saucepan with 250 ml of water, stir until dissolved, bring to the boil then leave to cool. Purée the diced melon together with the sugar syrup and the lime juice.

3 Place the sorbet in a shallow bowl and freeze for approx. 5 hours, stirring through thoroughly several times with a fork.

4 Beat the egg white with a pinch of salt until stiff. Fold into the sorbet and return to the freezer to harden. Scoop out with an ice cream scoop and serve.

Pomace sorbet
with sparkling wine

Serves 4
100 g sugar
juice of ½ a lime
150 ml Marc de
  Champagne
sparkling wine or fruit
  juice for pouring over

Preparation time: 20 minutes
  (plus cooling and freezing
  time)
Per serving approx.
  145 kcal/607 kJ
1 g P, 1 g F, 27 g CH

1 Place the sugar in a saucepan with 350 ml of water and stir until dissolved. Leave the syrup to cool. Stir the lime juice and the Marc de Champagne into the syrup.

2 Place the liquid in the freezer for approx. 6 hours, stirring through thoroughly several times. Using an ice cream scoop, place scoops of the sorbet in glasses and pour over the sparkling wine or fruit juice.

TIP

Marc de Champagne is a pomace brand from the Champagne region of France and is made from the residues of pressed grape. Only the grape varieties Pinot Noir, Pinot Meunier and Chardonnay are used to make Marc de Champagne.

Mango sorbet
with lime

Serves 4

2 untreated limes

1 ½ tsp powdered
   gelatine

1 mango

2 egg whites

1 tbsp icing sugar

Preparation time: 20 minutes
   (plus freezing time)

Per serving approx.
   67 kcal/281 kJ

4 g P, 2 g F, 7 g CH

1 Wash the limes under warm water and rub dry. Peel off a little of the zest for garnishing. Squeeze the juice. Stir three tablespoons of lime juice into the powdered gelatine and leave to swell.

2 Peel the mango, remove the flesh and dice. Purée the diced mango with 2 tablespoons of lime juice. Stir the gelatine over a bain-marie until it dissolves and stir into the mango purée.

3 Beat the egg whites with the sugar until stiff and fold into the mango mixture. Place the mixture in a shallow bowl and freeze for 4–5 hours, stirring through thoroughly several times with a fork.

4 Allow the sorbet to thaw slightly before serving and serve garnished with lemon zest.

Sophisticated sorbets

Rose petal sorbet
with white wine

Serves 4

225 ml white wine

juice of 1 lemon

50 g icing sugar

50 g powdered glucose

40 g untreated rose petals

Preparation time: 20 minutes
(plus infusing and freezing
time)

Per serving approx.
125 kcal/523 kJ
1 g P, 1 g F, 21 g CH

1 Combine the wine with 100 ml of water, the lemon juice and the sugar. Add the rose petals and leave to stand for approx. 24 hours. Strain the liquid through a sieve, squeezing the petals well.

2 Place in the freezer for approx. 4–5 hours, stirring through thoroughly several times with a fork. Divide the sorbet between dessert bowls.

TIP

In principle any rose variety can be used for the rose petal sorbet. The petals must not have been sprayed so use only untreated blossoms.

Pear and blackberry terrine
with honey

Serves 4

300 g pears
200 ml pear juice
1 tbsp honey
1 tsp vanilla essence
180 g blackberries,
   washed
1 tbsp powdered gelatine
2 egg whites

Preparation time: 40 minutes
   (plus cooling and freezing
   time)
Per serving approx.
   100 kcal/419 kJ
4 g P, 1 g F, 18 g CH

1 Peel the pears, remove the cores and dice the flesh. Place in a saucepan together with 100 ml of pear juice, bring to the boil and cook until soft. Add the honey and the vanilla essence, and purée. Blend ⅓ of the purée together with the blackberries then pass through a sieve. Put the rest of the purée aside.

2 Combine the powdered gelatine with 100 ml of the pear juice and stir until dissolved. Fold half of the gelatine-pear mixture into the pear purée previously set aside and fold the other half into the pear-blackberry purée. Leave both mixtures until cool and beginning to set.

3 Beat the egg whites until stiff. Fold half of the beaten egg whites into the pear purée and the other half into the pear-blackberry purée. Place in layers in a terrine mould and smooth over. Leave to freeze for approx. 4 hours. Allow to thaw slightly then slice and serve.

Melon sorbet
with sparkling wine

Serves 4

500 g watermelon

75 g sugar

2 tbsp lime

50 ml quince juice

375 ml sparkling wine

lemon balm leaves for
garnishing

Preparation time: 15 minutes
(plus drawing and freezing
time)
Per serving approx.
205 kcal/858 kJ
1 g P, 1 g F, 33 g CH

1 Peel the melon and remove the seeds, retaining the juice. Dice the flesh, combine with the sugar and leave to draw in the fridge for 30 minutes. Purée with the lime, quince and melon juices in a food processor.

2 Place in a shallow bowl and freeze for at least 6 hours, stirring through thoroughly several times. Serve using an ice cream scoop and place in sparkling wine glasses. Pour the sparkling wine over the sorbet and serve garnished with lemon balm.

Sophisticated sorbets

Blackberry sorbet
quick and easy

Serves 4

400 g frozen blackberries
4 tbsp sugar
2 tbsp lemon juice
2 tbsp raspberry syrup

Preparation time: 10 minutes
Per serving approx.
68 kcal/285 kJ
1 g P, 1 g F, 35 g CH

1 Purée the blackberries (still frozen) together with the sugar, lemon juice and raspberry syrup in a food processor until creamy. Place the sorbet in glasses and serve immediately.

TIP

Strictly speaking blackberries are not berries but an aggregate fruit belonging to the rose family. They are available from July to September. Wild blackberries are smaller but have more flavour than the cultivated varieties.

Elderflower sorbet
with sparkling wine

Serves 4

750 g sugar

½ untreated lemon, sliced

80 g elderflowers

350 ml sparkling wine

50 ml lemon juice

Preparation time: 20 minutes
  (plus cooking, cooling and
  freezing time)
Per serving approx.
  868 kcal/3634 kJ
1 g P, 1 g F, 196 g CH

1 Combine 500 ml of water with the sugar and lemon slices, and bring to the boil, stirring until the sugar has dissolved. Simmer for 3 minutes. Rinse the elderflowers, shake dry and place in the syrup. Bring back to the boil.

2 Strain through a sieve and leave to cool. Measure out 175 ml from the elderflower syrup, combine with the sparkling wine and the lemon juice, place in a shallow container and freeze for 4–5 hours. Garnish the sorbet as desired and serve.

Peach sorbet
with Prosecco

Serves 4

1.5 kg pears

1 lemon

2 cl pear schnapps

2 leaves white gelatine

Prosecco to serve

Preparation time: 20 minutes
(plus softening and freezing
time)

Per serving approx.
61 kcal/255 kJ

1 g P, 1 g F, 7 g CH

1 Wash the pears, cut into quarters, remove the cores and dice the flesh. Squeeze the lemon and drizzle the juice over the pears. Purée the pears and pass the purée through a sieve. Stir in the pear schnapps.

2 Soften the gelatine in cold water for 10 minutes, squeeze the water out and dissolve in a little water over a medium heat. Fold into the pear purée.

3 Place the mixture in a shallow bowl in the freezer for approx. 4 hours, stirring through thoroughly several times so that the sorbet stays creamy. Using an ice cream scoop, place the sorbet in glasses and pour over the Prosecco.

TIP

Pear juice can be used instead of Prosecco if preferred.

Grape sorbet
with figs

Serves 4

400 g sweet white grapes
2 tbsp sugar
1 tsp powdered glucose
2 small figs
fig slivers for garnishing

Preparation time: 20 minutes
(plus freezing time)
Per serving approx.
92 kcal/385 kJ
1 g P, 1 g F, 21 g CH

1 Wash the grapes and pat dry. Place the sugar in a saucepan with 100 ml of water and stir until the sugar has dissolved. Bring to the boil and simmer for approx. 5 minutes. Stir in the powdered glucose, add the grapes and purée the mixture. Pass through a sieve then place in a shallow container.

2 Peel the figs and dice finely. Fold into the grape mixture and freeze for approx. 4 hours, stirring through carefully several times. Serve in scoops garnished with figs.

Passion fruit sorbet
fruity fresh

Serves 4

2–3 passion fruit
750 ml orange juice
125 g icing sugar
2 egg whites
salt
segments and zest from
  1 untreated orange for
  garnishing

Preparation time: 20 minutes
  (plus freezing time)
Per serving approx.
  219 kcal/917 kJ
5 g P, 1 g F, 44 g CH

1 Slice open the passion fruit, scoop out the flesh and weigh out 185 g. Combine with the orange juice and icing sugar and place in the freezer until half frozen. Mix in a food processor and freeze again for another 3 hours.

2 Beat the egg whites with a pinch of salt until stiff, fold into the sorbet mixture and return to the freezer to harden. Use an ice cream scoop to place the sorbet in dessert bowls and garnish as desired with orange segments and zest from the untreated orange.

Fruits of the forest sorbet
with orange and pear juice

Serves 4

200 ml blood orange juice

75 ml pear juice

5 tbsp sugar

400 g mixed fruits of the
  forest

1 tbsp lime juice

Preparation time: 20 minutes
  (plus cooking, cooling and
  freezing time)
Per serving approx.
  106 kcal/444 kJ
1 g P, 1 g F, 22 g CH

1 Mix the blood orange juice with the pear juice and the sugar in a saucepan. Stir until the sugar has dissolved, bring to the boil and simmer for approx. 3 minutes until syrupy. Leave to cool completely. Wash the fruits of the forest, drain, purée and mix into the syrup. Season with a little lime juice to taste.

2 Place the mixture in a bowl and freeze for approx. 6 hours, stirring through thoroughly every hour. Whizz the sorbet in a food processor until smooth, place in a piping bag and pipe decoratively into glasses.

Lighter treats with yoghurt

Kiwi fruit ice cream
with buttermilk

Serves 4

5 kiwi fruits (approx. 250 g)
1 tbsp lemon juice
50 g sugar
1 tbsp acacia honey
50 g white chocolate
200 ml buttermilk
kiwi fruit slices and mixed
   fruit for garnishing

Preparation time: 20 minutes
   (plus cooling and freezing
   time)
Per serving approx.
   180 kcal/754 kJ
3 g P, 4 g F, 30 g CH

1 Peel the kiwi fruit, dice and mix together with the lemon juice. Purée with a hand blender and combine with the sugar and 2 cl of water. Transfer to a saucepan and bring to the boil; simmer, stirring, for 3 minutes. Pass through a sieve, stir in the honey and leave to cool.

2 Melt the white chocolate in a bain-marie. Combine with the buttermilk and the kiwi fruit mixture. Pour into a shallow bowl and freeze for approx. 6 hours, stirring thoroughly several times. Divide into portions and serve garnished with kiwi fruit slices and mixed fruit.

Blackberry ice cream
with yoghurt

Serves 4

250 g blackberries

5 tbsp sugar

2 eggs

150 g yoghurt

berries of your choice for
    garnishing

Preparation time: 20 minutes
    (plus freezing time)
Per serving approx.
    115 kcal/481 kJ
5 g P, 5 g F, 9 g CH

1 Wash the blackberries and leave to drain. Purée with 2 tablespoons of sugar and pass through a sieve.

2 Beat the eggs together with the rest of the sugar until creamy, then gradually fold in the berry purée and the yoghurt.

3 Place the mixture in a freezer for approx. 6 hours. Serve garnished with the berries of your choice.

TIP

"Yoghurt" is derived from a Turkish word and literally means "fermented milk". Yoghurt is made from thickened milk using lactic acid bacteria and is sour in taste. It is available as skimmed (up to 0.5% fat), low fat (1.5–1.8% fat), normal (min. 3.5% fat) and creamy yoghurt (min. 10% fat).

Crunchy yoghurt ice cream
with walnuts

Serves 4

175 g bread
25 g chopped walnuts
5 tbsp sugar
½ tsp grated nutmeg
1 tsp grated zest from
  1 untreated orange
450 g yoghurt
2 egg whites
slices from 1 untreated
  orange for decoration

Preparation time: 20 minutes
  (plus browning, cooling and
  freezing time)
Per serving approx.
  217 kcal/909 kJ
9 g P, 8 g F, 24 g CH

1 Crumble the bread and combine with the walnuts and the sugar. Spread out over a baking sheet lined with aluminium foil and brown under a hot grill for approx. 5 minutes until golden. Stir several times and leave to cool.

2 Combine the crunchy mixture with the nutmeg, orange zest and the yoghurt. Beat the egg whites until stiff and fold into the mixture. Place in dessert bowls and freeze for approx. 4 hours. Tip the ice cream out of the bowls and serve garnished with orange slices.

Quark honey ice cream
with vanilla

Serves 4

200 g acacia honey
350 ml milk
1 vanilla pod
250 g low fat quark (soft
  cheese)
raspberries and honey
  for decoration

Preparation time: 15 minutes
  (plus cooling and freezing
  time)
Per serving approx.
  263 kcal/1101 kJ
12 g P, 3 g F, 45 g CH

1 Combine the honey with the milk in a saucepan. Slice open the vanilla pod, scrape out the seeds and add pod and seeds to the milk and honey. Bring the mixture to the boil then leave to cool in a cold bain-marie.

2 Remove the pod and mix the vanilla milk together with the quark in a food processor until smooth. Transfer the mixture into a bowl and freeze for 5–6 hours, until solid, stirring carefully several times in order to break up the ice crystals.

3 Use an ice cream scoop to distribute among dessert bowls and serve garnished with raspberries and honey.

Blueberry ice cream
with ricotta

Serves 4

200 g blueberries
2 tbsp lemon juice
75 g icing sugar
100 g ricotta
100 ml milk
30 g vanilla sugar
½ tsp vanilla seeds

Preparation time: 30 minutes
  (plus cooling and freezing
  time)
Per serving approx.
  110 kcal/461 kJ
4 g P, 3 g F, 16 g CH

1 Wash the blueberries and leave to drain. Purée together with the lemon juice and the icing sugar, and place in the freezer for approx. 15 minutes.

2 Mix the ricotta with a little milk until smooth. Combine with the rest of the milk, the vanilla sugar and the vanilla seeds, place in a saucepan and bring to the boil. Leave to cool in a cold bain-marie then combine with the fruit purée.

3 Place the mixture in a shallow bowl and freeze for approx. 6 hours, stirring through thoroughly several times. Thaw slightly before serving.

TIP

Wild blueberries are much smaller, but far more aromatic than the cultivated varieties. Their flesh is dark violet in colour. Beware of the fox tapeworm when gathering wild blueberries yourself!

Lighter treats with yoghurt

Passion fruit ice cream
with yoghurt

Serves 4

6 passion fruit
200 g yoghurt
2 egg yolks
20 g sugar
pomegranate seeds for
  decorating

Preparation time: 15 minutes
  (plus freezing time)
Per serving approx.
  241 kcal/1009 kJ
7 g P, 6 g F, 32 g CH

1 Cut the passion fruit in half, scoop out the pulp with a spoon and combine with the yoghurt in a bowl.

2 Beat the egg yolks with the sugar until creamy and fold into the passion fruit yoghurt mixture. Place in a shallow bowl and freeze for approx. 1 hour.

3 Mix the ice cream through until creamy. Freeze for a further 5 hours. Remove from the freezer 10 minutes before serving to allow to thaw a little. Use an ice cream scoop to place in glasses and serve the ice cream garnished with pomegranate seeds.

Rhubarb ice cream
with yoghurt

Serves 4

350 g rhubarb

75 g strawberries

125 g sugar

125 g full fat yoghurt

rhubarb compote as
desired

Preparation time: 30 minutes
(plus cooking, cooling and
freezing time)

Per serving approx.
165 kcal/691 kJ

2 g P, 1 g F, 35 g CH

1 Wash and peel the rhubarb, and chop roughly.
Wash the strawberries and cut in half. Place in a
saucepan together with the rhubarb, the sugar and
125 ml of water, bring to the boil and simmer for approx.
15 minutes. Leave to cool.

2 Purée the fruit mixture then pass through a sieve.
Stir in the yoghurt. Place in individual glasses and
freeze for approx. 6 hours, stirring through thoroughly
several times. Allow to thaw slightly before serving
together with rhubarb compote as desired.

TIP

The rhubarb season begins mid-April and lasts until the
end of June. Rhubarb continues growing until later in
the year, but it should no longer be eaten because the
levels of oxalic acid are then too high which make it dif-
ficult to digest. These levels are reduced by cooking, but
it is still advisable to peel the rhubarb.

Honey ice cream
with double cream

Serves 4

3 egg yolks
75 g blossom honey
100 ml fat-free milk
125 g double cream
honey and fresh fruit for
    decorating

Preparation time: 20 minutes
    (plus cooling and freezing
    time)
Per serving approx.
    196 kcal/821 kJ
3 g P, 13 g F, 16 g CH

1 Beat the egg yolks together with the blossom honey until foamy. Heat the fat-free milk and stir into the egg mixture. Heat the mixture, stirring all the time, until it thickens, making sure that it does not boil.

2 Place the cream in a metal bowl over a cold bain-marie and leave to cool. Place in the freezer to freeze for approx. 6 hours, stirring through thoroughly several times.

3 Whip the double cream until frothy and fold into the ice cream 20 minutes before the end of the freezing. Use an ice cream scoop to place on plates. Drizzle with a little honey and garnish with fresh fruit.

Almond amaretto ice cream
with double cream

Serves 4

100 g almond slivers
1 vanilla pod
250 ml fat-free milk
2 egg yolks
70 g sugar
125 g double cream
1 tbsp amaretto

Preparation time: 40 minutes
(plus browning, infusing,
cooling and freezing time)
Per serving approx.
250 kcal/1047 kJ
6 g P, 18 g F, 15 g CH

1 Dry fry the almond slivers and leave to cool. Cut open the vanilla pod, scrape out the seeds, stir into the milk and bring to the boil. Remove from the heat, cover and leave to infuse for 20 minutes.

2 Re-heat the vanilla milk. Beat the egg yolks with the sugar until foamy and stir in 3 tablespoons of the hot vanilla milk. Gradually add the rest of the milk, stirring all the time until the mixture thickens, but do not allow it to boil. Place in a metal bowl over an ice cold bain-marie and stir until cold.

3 Freeze for approx. 6 hours, stirring a couple of times. Whip the double cream until foamy. Fold half of the almond slivers together with the amaretto and the double cream into the ice cream mixture approx. 1 hour before the end of the freezing time. Serve the ice cream garnished with the remaining almond slivers.

Cinnamon ice cream
with gingerbread crumbs

Serves 6

2 fresh egg yolks
125 g icing sugar
200 g double cream
250 g low-fat yoghurt
2 level tsp cinnamon
60 g gingerbread (without
icing)

Preparation time: 20 minutes
(plus freezing and cooking
time)
Per serving approx.
350 kcal/1460 kJ
4 g E, 25 g F, 28 g KH

1 Beat the egg yolks and the sugar over a hot bain-marie for approx. 10 minutes until pale and creamy. Leave to cool slightly.

2 Fold in the double cream, yoghurt and cinnamon. Finely crumble the gingerbread and fold into the mixture. Place the ice cream mixture in 6 moulds (approx. 150 ml each) and smooth the surface. Cover and freeze overnight.

3 Dip the moulds briefly in hot water and either tip the ice cream onto dessert plates or serve in the moulds.

TIP

Serve the cinnamon ice cream with mulled plums. Drain 1 jar of plums (720 g), retaining the juice. Bring the juice to the boil together with 2 pinches of ground cloves and ground aniseed. Combine a little red wine with a little cornflour, stir into the juice and bring to the boil. Fold in the plums.

Lime ice cream
with yoghurt and quark

Serves 4

2 untreated limes
250 g natural yoghurt
250 g quark (40 %)
150 ml milk
80 g sugar
30 g vanilla sugar

Preparation time: 10 minutes
  (plus freezing time)
Per serving approx.
  320 kcal/1330 kJ
8 g P, 16 g F, 45 g CH

1 Wash the limes under warm water and rub dry. Finely grate the zest and squeeze out the juice. Place the natural yoghurt in a mixing bowl with the quark, milk, sugar and vanilla sugar, lime zest and lime juice, and mix with a hand blender.

2 Place the yoghurt mixture in a suitable bowl (ideally stainless steel) and freeze for approx. 5 hours, mixing through again with a hand blender after 1 hour. This step is not necessary if you are using an ice cream maker. Let the ice cream thaw slightly before serving in scoops.

TIP

This ice cream also tastes really good with sparkling wine! Place a scoop in each tall glass and top up with sparkling wine.

Papaya quark ice cream
with ginger

Serves 4

1 ripe papaya
1 piece ginger
  (approx. 1 cm)
2 limes
1–2 oranges
250 g brown sugar
150 ml milk
150 g quark (40 %)

Preparation time: 30 minutes
  (plus freezing time)
Per serving approx.
  390 kcal/1630 kJ
5 g P, 9 g F, 71 g CH

1 Peel the papaya, cut in half and remove the pips. Dice the flesh and purée with a hand blender until smooth (you will need approx. 300 g of puréed papaya). Peel the ginger, dice finely and add to the papaya. Purée again.

2 Squeeze the juice from the limes and the oranges. Place 3 tablespoons of lime juice with 100 ml of orange juice and the brown sugar in a bowl, and stir until the sugar has completely dissolved.

3 Add the rest of the orange juice to the papaya-ginger mixture, stir in the milk and the quark, and place in a suitable bowl (ideally stainless steel). Leave in the freezer for 1 hour and mix again with the hand blender. Freeze again for a further 4 hours at least.

Blackberry ice cream
with quark

Serves 4

300 g blackberries

100 g sugar

1 vanilla pod

350 g quark (20 %)

100 ml milk

Preparation time: 15 minutes
  (plus freezing time)
Per serving approx.
  260 kcal/1080 kJ
10 g P, 11 g F, 31 g CH

1 Wash the blackberries and pat dry. Place in a bowl with the sugar and purée with a hand blender until creamy.

2 Slice open the vanilla pod with a sharp knife, scrape out the seeds and add to the blackberries together with the quark and the milk. Whisk together thoroughly and pour into a suitable mould (ideally stainless steel). Leave in the freezer for 1 hour, purée again and freeze again for a further 4 hours.

TIP

Using low fat quark and mineral water will make the recipe particularly low in calories. Beat the quark together with 100 ml of mineral water until smooth and mix together with the blackberries.

Lemon cream ice cream
with buttermilk

Serves 4

3 lemons
100 ml cream
300 ml buttermilk
200 g sour cream
200 g sugar

Preparation time: 10 minutes
(plus freezing time)
Per serving approx.
440 kcal/1830 kJ
5 g P, 18 g F, 63 g CH

1 Squeeze the juice from the lemons. Whip the cream until stiff. Combine the lemon juice with the buttermilk, sour cream and the sugar until the sugar crystals have dissolved. Fold in the whipped cream.

2 Place the mixture in a suitable bowl (ideally stainless steel) and leave in the freezer for 1 hour. Stir through with a fork then freeze again for at least another 4 hours.

TIP

Ideally, the cream needs to be cold for it to whip up stiffly. The mixing bowl and the whisks from the hand mixer should also be well chilled. If the room temperature is too warm, as in summer for example, the cream may fail to whip up stiffly and curdle instead.

Espresso ricotta ice cream
with Sambuca

Serves 4

125 ml freshly brewed
  espresso coffee
500 g ricotta
4 egg yolks
120 g sugar
100 ml cream
4 tbsp Sambuca
chocolate-covered coffee
  beans for garnishing

Preparation time: 15 minutes
  (plus draining and freezing
  time)
Per serving approx.
  510 kcal/2130 kJ
16 g P, 33 g F, 31 g CH

1 Leave the espresso to cool completely. Drain the ricotta in a sieve and combine with the espresso, mixing until smooth.

2 In a second bowl, beat the egg yolks with the sugar until pale yellow and frothy. In a third bowl, whip the cream until stiff.

3 Fold the ricotta espresso mixture into the egg yolk mixture, then add the cream and the Sambuca according to taste.

4 Place the mixture in the freezer and freeze for at least 5 hours. Serve the ice cream garnished with chocolate-covered coffee beans.

TIP

Ricotta is an Italian whey cheese made from sheep or cow milk whey. A special but rare delicacy is ricotta di bufala, made from buffalo milk whey.

Sinfully smooth with cream and milk

Coffee ice cream
with double cream

Serves 6

300 ml milk

2 tbsp sugar

1 tbsp instant coffee

1 egg

2 egg yolks

300 ml double cream

50 g chopped cashew nuts

Preparation time: 20 minutes
(plus cooling and freezing
time)

Per serving approx.
272 kcal/1139 kJ
7 g P, 24 g F, 8 g CH

1 Heat the milk in a saucepan with 1 tbsp of sugar, stirring until the sugar has dissolved. Bring to the boil, remove from the heat and stir in the coffee powder.

2 Beat the egg and the egg yolks over a hot bain-marie until foamy. Add to the milk-coffee mixture and stir over the bain-marie until creamy, but do not allow to boil. Leave to cool.

3 Beat the double cream with the rest of the sugar until half stiff and fold into the coffee cream together with the cashew nuts.

4 Transfer the mixture into a shallow container and freeze for approx. 4–5 hours, stirring several times.

Sinfully smooth with cream and milk

Cardamom milk ice cream
with almonds and pistachio nuts

Serves 4

1 l milk
6 whole cardamom pods
3 tbsp icing sugar
15 g chopped almonds
15 g chopped pistachio
  nuts

Preparation time: 20 minutes
  (plus cooling and freezing
  time)
Per serving approx.
  214 kcal/896 kJ
10 g P, 13 g F, 15 g CH

1 Add the cardamom pods to the milk in a saucepan and bring to the boil. Reduce the heat and simmer, stirring all the time, until the milk has reduced by ⅔. Add the sugar and simmer for 2 minutes. Remove the cardamom pods. Add the almonds and pistachio nuts, transfer to a shallow container and leave to cool.

2 Freeze for approx. 5 hours, stirring thoroughly several times to break up the ice crystals. Divide the ice cream into individual moulds and freeze overnight. Tip out of the moulds to serve.

Sinfully smooth with cream and milk

Lemongrass ice cream
with maple syrup

Serves 4

150 g lemongrass
100 ml lemon juice
80 g icing sugar
300 g maple syrup
2 tsp powdered glucose
200 ml milk
150 ml cream
grated zest of 1 untreated
  lemon
fruit of your choice for
  serving

Preparation time: 20 minutes
  (plus infusing and freezing
  time)
Per serving approx.
  478 kcal/2001 kJ
3 g P, 13 g F, 83 g CH

1 Wash the lemongrass, cut in half lengthways and cut into pieces. Combine in a saucepan together with the lemon juice and the sugar, and bring to the boil. Remove the saucepan from the heat, stir in the maple syrup and powdered glucose, and leave to cool. Stir in the milk and leave to infuse for 2 hours.

2 Pass the mixture through a sieve. Whip the cream until stiff and fold into the mixture. Transfer to a shallow bowl and freeze for approx. 6 hours, stirring thoroughly several times. Serve in scoops with the fruits of your choice.

Sinfully smooth with cream and milk

Walnut ice cream
simply great

Serves 4

50 g walnuts

500 ml milk

5 egg yolks

100 g icing sugar

Preparation time: 20 minutes
  (plus infusing, cooling and
  freezing time)
Per serving approx.
  308 kcal/1290 kJ
10 g P, 21 g F, 20 g CH

1 Shell the walnuts and chop them. Bring the milk to the boil, remove from the heat and add the walnuts, leaving them to infuse for approx. 10 minutes.

2 Beat the egg yolks with the icing sugar until foamy. Add to the nut milk and stir over a hot bain-marie until creamy. Cool over a cold bain-marie, stirring all the time.

3 Transfer the mixture into a shallow bowl and freeze for approx. 6 hours, stirring thoroughly several times. Thaw slightly before serving.

Sinfully smooth with cream and milk

Ice cream pudding
with glacé fruit

Serves 5

25 g chopped, roasted
  almonds
20 g candied lemon peel
30 g raisins
30 g sultanas
30 g currants
40 ml rum
500 ml stracciatella
  ice cream (see p. 152,
  without the chocolate
  pieces)
50 g red and green glacé
  cherries
1 tsp ground cinnamon
½ tsp ground nutmeg
500 ml chocolate ice cream
  (see p. 131)

Preparation time: 20 minutes
  (plus infusing and freezing
  times)
Per serving approx.
  628 kcal/2629 kJ
  3 g P, 28 g F, 82 g CH

1 Place the almonds, candied lemon peel, raisins, sultanas and currants in a bowl and pour over the rum. Leave to infuse overnight.

2 Thaw the stracciatella ice cream slightly. Chop the glacé cherries and fold into the ice cream. Line a small pudding mould with cling film and spread the ice cream over the base of the mould. Freeze for 6 hours.

3 Combine the soaked fruit with the spices and fold into the chocolate ice cream. Spread this mixture over the frozen stracciatella ice cream and freeze overnight.

4 Tip the ice cream pudding out of the mould, remove the cling film and cut into slices.

Chocolate ice cream
with dark chocolate

Serves 4

2 egg yolks
30 g vanilla sugar
75 g sugar
125 ml milk
75 g dark chocolate
175 ml cream
1 tsp cocoa powder

Preparation time: 20 minutes
(plus cooling and freezing
time)

Per serving approx.
300 kcal/1256 kJ
7 g P, 18 g F, 26 g CH

1 Beat the egg yolks with the vanilla sugar until foamy, then gradually add the sugar. Place the milk in a saucepan and bring to the boil. Slowly whisk into the egg mixture, stirring all the time. Return to the saucepan and re-heat, stirring all the time, until it thickens but do not allow to boil.

2 Remove from the heat. Melt the dark chocolate together with 3 tablespoons of cream over a hot bain-marie, stirring all the time. Stir in the cocoa powder and combine with the egg and milk mixture. Chill for approx. 30 minutes.

3 Whip the rest of the cream until stiff and fold into the chocolate mixture. Divide among the dessert bowls or glasses and freeze for approx. 6 hours. Serve garnished with grated chocolate.

Sinfully smooth with cream and milk   131

Lychee ice cream
with glacé ginger

Serves 4

200 g fresh lychees
1 tbsp lemon juice
3 tbsp icing sugar
10 g glacé ginger
200 ml milk
150 ml cream
gooseberries and grated
  chocolate for garnishing

Preparation time: 30 minutes
  (plus cooling and freezing
  time)
Per serving approx.
  295 kcal/1235 kJ
6 g P, 19 g F, 23 g CH

1 Peel the lychees, remove the pips and dice the flesh. Combine with the lemon juice and purée. Stir in the icing sugar and chill.

2 Finely chop the ginger and place half of it in a saucepan together with the milk. Bring to the boil and remove from the heat. Strain the milk and cool over a cold bain-marie, stirring all the time. Combine with the lychee purée. Whip the cream until stiff and fold into the lychee mixture.

3 Place in a shallow bowl and freeze for 2 hours. Stir through, fold in the rest of the diced ginger and freeze again for a further 4 hours. Thaw slightly prior to serving and serve garnished with gooseberries and grated chocolate according to taste.

Orange ice cream
with Cointreau

Serves 4

5 untreated oranges

100 g tinned mandarin
  oranges

50 g sugar

2 tbsp Cointreau

150 ml ricotta

200 ml cream

fruit sauce according to
  taste for garnishing

Preparation time: 20 minutes
  (plus freezing time)
Per serving approx.
  355 kcal/1486 kJ
8 g P, 18 g F, 37 g CH

1 Wash the oranges under warm water, rub dry and then finely grate the zest from 1 orange. Segment the flesh of all the oranges, retaining the juice to use in another recipe. Drain the tinned mandarin oranges.

2 Purée the orange segments together with the mandarin oranges and the sugar, and pass through a sieve. Stir the Cointreau, ricotta and orange zest into the purée.

3 Beat the cream until stiff and fold into the mixture. Place in a shallow container and freeze for 5–6 hours.

4 Thaw slightly, place in a piping bag and pipe decoratively into dessert bowls or ice cream cones. Garnish with fruit sauce according to taste.

Sinfully smooth with cream and milk

Peach maracuya ice cream
with sour milk

Serves 4

2 maracuyas

2 peaches

1 tsp lime juice

100 g blossom honey

200 ml sour milk

100 ml cream

zest from 1 untreated lime
for garnishing

Preparation time: 20 minutes
(plus cooling, cooking and
freezing time)
Per serving approx.
255 kcal/1068 kJ
4 g P, 10 g F, 35 g CH

1 Cut the maracuyas in half and scoop out the pulp. Wash the peaches, remove their skin, cut them in half, remove the stones and dice the flesh. Purée both types of fruit with the lime juice and pass through a sieve.

2 Place the residue left in the sieve in a saucepan together with 2 tablespoons of honey and 2 tablespoons of water, and simmer for approx. 5 minutes. Sieve again and leave to cool. Add to the fruit purée and freeze.

3 Combine the rest of the honey with the sour milk in a saucepan, bring to the boil and reduce until creamy. Leave to cool over a cold bain-marie then stir into the frozen fruit purée.

4 Whip the cream until stiff and fold into the mixture. Place in a shallow bowl and freeze for 5–6 hours, stirring through several times. Thaw slightly before serving. Garnish with lime zest.

Basil ice cream
with balsamic strawberries

Serves 4

1 vanilla pod
250 ml cream
250 ml fat-free milk
2 eggs
2 egg yolks
110 g sugar
juice and zest from
  1 untreated lemon
30 g basil leaves
80 ml balsamic vinegar
100 ml sweet sherry
100 g strawberries
basil leaves for garnishing

Preparation time: 30 minutes
  (plus cooling and freezing
  time)
Per serving approx.
  297 kcal/1243 kJ
10 g P, 13 g F, 25 g CH

1 Scoop the seeds out of the vanilla pod, place in a saucepan together with the cream and 200 ml of milk. Bring to the boil and leave to infuse for 30 minutes. Beat the eggs with the egg yolks and 75 g of the sugar until creamy. Slowly stir in the warm vanilla milk. Return to the saucepan and re-heat, stirring all the time, until the mixture thickens, but do not allow it to boil. Strain through a sieve, stir in the lemon juice and zest and leave to cool.

2 Purée the washed basil leaves with the rest of the milk. Stir into the ice cream mixture, pour into a bowl and freeze for at least 6 hours, stirring through every now and again.

3 For the balsamic strawberries, place the rest of the sugar in a frying pan and caramelise, stirring all the time. Deglaze with the balsamic vinegar and pour in the sherry. Simmer over a medium heat until syrupy then leave to cool. Wash the strawberries, pat dry and cut into quarters. Arrange on plates and add 1–2 scoops of basil ice cream. Drizzle the balsamic vinegar reduction over the strawberries and serve garnished with basil leaves.

Sinfully smooth with cream and milk

Apricot ice cream
with rosemary

Serves 6

400 ml cream

100 ml milk

4 egg yolks

125 g sugar

500 g apricots

1 tbsp lemon juice

½ vanilla pod

½ tsp finely chopped
  rosemary

Preparation time: 20 minutes
  (plus cooling and freezing
  time)

Per serving approx.
  375 kcal/1570 kJ
5 g P, 25 g F, 31 g CH

1 Place the cream in a saucepan together with the milk, heat, then remove from the stove. Beat the egg yolks together with 100 g of the sugar until foamy and stir into the hot milk. Return to the heat, stirring all the time, until the mixture thickens, but do not allow it to boil. Leave to cool.

2 Skin the apricots, cut them in half and remove the stones. Purée the flesh together with the lemon juice, the rest of the sugar and the seeds scraped out of the vanilla pod. Stir the rosemary into the fruit purée. Stir the cream and milk mixture into the fruit mixture, place in a shallow container and freeze for 5–6, stirring through several times.

3 Place the apricot ice cream in dessert bowls and serve immediately, accompanied by a fruit sauce according to taste.

Sicilian Cassata
classic ice cream

Serves 10

6 eggs

110 g icing sugar

430 ml cream

50 g chopped and roasted
almonds

130 g dark chocolate

1 tbsp cocoa powder

125 g cream cheese

250 g glacé fruit of your
choice

2 tsp cherry liqueur

fruit sauce for decorating

Preparation time: 50 minutes
(plus freezing times)
Per serving approx.
399 kcal/1671 kJ
9 g P, 26 g F, 31 g CH

1 Separate the eggs and beat 2 egg whites with 40 g of the icing sugar until stiff. Whip 185 ml of the cream until stiff. Beat 2 egg yolks until creamy then combine with the cream and the whisked egg whites. Fold in the almonds.

2 Line a square cake tin (approx. 20 x 20 cm) with cling film. Place the mixture in the tin and freeze for approx. 1 hour.

3 Roughly chop the chocolate and melt over a hot bain-marie, stirring all the time. Stir in the cocoa powder and leave to cool slightly. Repeat the process described above with 2 egg whites, 2 egg yolks, 40 g icing sugar and 185 ml of cream.

4 Spread the mixture over the frozen first layer and freeze for another 60 minutes. Do the same again as described above with the remaining eggs, cream and icing sugar, stirring the cream cheese into this mixture. Finely chop the candied fruit and fold into the mixture together with the cherry liqueur.

5 Spread the mixture over the frozen chocolate layer, cover with cling film and freeze overnight. Cut the cassata into slices and serve with a fruit sauce.

Mint ice cream
with sour milk

Serves 4

300 ml cream

300 ml sour milk

seeds from 1 vanilla pod

8 egg yolks

75 g icing sugar

4 tbsp freshly chopped
mint leaves

fruit sauce for decorating

Preparation time: 30 minutes
(plus cooling and freezing
time)

Per serving approx.
510 kcal/2135 kJ
13 g P, 42 g F, 20 g CH

1 Combine the cream and sour milk with the vanilla seeds in a saucepan and heat, but do not boil. Beat the egg yolks with the icing sugar until foamy. Stir the cream and sour milk into the egg mixture, stirring all the time, and beat until loose folds form. Add the mint leaves and to cool.

2 Place the mixture in a shallow bowl and freeze for approx. 6 hours, stirring through several times. Thaw slightly before serving. Use an ice cream scoop to serve accompanied by a fruit sauce.

Sinfully smooth with cream and milk

Vanilla–blueberry bombe
with glacé fruit

Serves 6

225 g frozen blueberries

150 ml orange juice

zest of 1 untreated orange

½ tsp allspice

50 g sugar

500 ml vanilla ice cream
(see p. 229)

2 tbsp mixed glacé fruit

1 tbsp roasted flaked
almonds

Preparation time: 25 minutes
(plus cooling and freezing
time)

Per serving approx.
222 kcal/929 kJ

4 g P, 8 g F, 23 g CH

1 Thaw the blueberries. Place in a saucepan with the orange juice, orange zest and allspice, and bring to the boil. Add the sugar and purée the berries. Leave the purée to cool.

2 Thaw the vanilla ice cream slightly. Chop the glacé fruit and fold into the ice cream together with the almonds.

3 Place the vanilla mixture in a pudding mould lined with cling film. Shape a hollow in the middle of the mixture with a spoon. Place the ice cream in the freezer to set.

4 Pour the blueberry sorbet into the hollow and freeze again until hardened. Tip the ice cream out of the mould, remove the cling film and slice the ice cream bombe.

Sinfully smooth with cream and milk

Hazelnut ice cream
with hazelnut liqueur

Serves 4

75 g hazelnuts

75 g sugar

475 ml milk

1 vanilla pod

4 egg yolks

2 cl hazelnut liqueur

Preparation time: 30 minutes
  (plus cooling and freezing
  time)
Per serving approx.
  360 kcal/1507 kJ
10 g P, 23 g F, 28 g CH

1 Dry fry the hazelnuts in a saucepan, then leave to cool. Rub off the skins. Combine the nuts with 2 tablespoons of sugar and grind.

2 Place the milk in a saucepan, slice open the vanilla pod, scrape out the seeds and add them, together with the pod, to the milk. Heat until just before boiling point then remove the vanilla pod.

3 Beat the egg yolks until foamy, combine with the hot milk and the rest of the sugar over a hot bain-marie, and stir until creamy. Stir in the nuts and the liqueur and leave to cool.

4 Place in a shallow bowl and freeze for approx. 6 hours, stirring through thoroughly several times. Serve in scoops.

Sinfully smooth with cream and milk

Caramel ice cream
with calvados

Serves 6

300 g sugar

150 ml milk

4 egg yolks

2 cl calvados

2 egg whites

350 ml cream

fruit sauce or chocolate
  sauce for serving

Preparation time: 30 minutes
  (plus cooling, cooking and
  freezing time)
Per serving approx.
  455 kcal/1905 kJ
6 g P, 23 g F, 53 g CH

1 Heat 200 g of the sugar in a frying pan and cara-melise, stirring all the time. Pour in the milk and slowly bring to the boil, stirring all the time. Leave to cool.

2 Beat the egg yolks until foamy and combine with the caramel milk. Stir over a hot bain-marie until creamy. Place over a cold bain-marie and stir until cold. Stir in the calvados.

3 Combine the rest of the sugar with 100 ml of water, bring to the boil and simmer until syrupy. Beat the egg whites until soft peaks form and combine with the sugar syrup. Leave to cool slightly then fold into the caramel mixture. Whip the cream until stiff and fold in.

4 Place the mixture in mould lined with cling film and freeze for 6–7 hours. Tip out of the mould and cut into slices. Serve with a fruit or chocolate sauce.

Sinfully smooth with cream and milk

Stracciatella ice cream
classic and so good

Serves 4

100 g white chocolate

200 ml milk

200 ml cream

50 g dark chocolate,
  chopped

Preparation time: 20 minutes
  (plus cooling and freezing
  time)

Per serving approx.
  378 kcal/1583 kJ
  5 g P, 28 g F, 26 g CH

1 Roughly chop the white chocolate, combine with the milk and 100 ml of the cream over a hot bain-marie, and stir until the chocolate has melted. Mix in a food processor until smooth and leave to cool. Whip the rest of the cream until stiff then fold into the mixture.

2 Place the mixture in a shallow mould and freeze for 2 hours. Fold the dark chocolate into the white chocolate mixture and freeze again for another 4 hours. Serve in scoops.

TIP

Chocolate is available with a variety of different cocoa contents. The higher the proportion of cocoa the darker, more flavourful and more bitter the chocolate is. White chocolate, on the other hand, has no cocoa at all and contains only cocoa butter, sugar, powdered milk and flavourings, usually vanilla. It has a very high sugar content of over 50%.

White chocolate ice cream
with almond brittle

Serves 4

70 g roasted almonds

2 tbsp sugar

185 ml cream

60 g icing sugar

125 g white chocolate

250 g mascarpone

fat for greasing

fruit for garnishing

Preparation time: 20 minutes
(plus cooling and freezing
time)

Per serving approx.
658 kcal/2755 kJ

13 g P, 53 g F, 35 g CH

1 Line a baking tray with aluminium foil and grease lightly. Place the almonds on the tray. Caramelise the sugar in a saucepan and pour over the almonds. Leave to cool. Break the almond brittle into pieces then crush in a plastic bag using a rolling pin.

2 Whip the cream with the icing sugar until stiff. Melt the white chocolate in a saucepan, stirring all the time. Leave to cool slightly and then mix with mascarpone. Fold in the cream.

3 Place the mixture in a shallow mould, cover and freeze over night. Serve the ice cream in scoops sprinkled with the almond brittle. Serve with the fruit of your choice.

Chocolate ice cream
with whisky

Serves 6

250 g dark chocolate
60 g butter
4 egg yolks
315 ml cream
¼ tsp ground vanilla
2 tbsp whisky
desiccated coconut for
   garnishing

Preparation time: 20 minutes
   (plus cooling and freezing
   time)
Per serving approx.
   452 kcal/1892 kJ
9 g P, 37 g F, 21 g CH

1 Roughly chop the chocolate and melt over a hot bain-marie, stirring all the time, then leave to cool slightly. Beat the butter will creamy and fold into the chocolate. Combine the cream with the vanilla and beat until stiff. Fold into the chocolate mixture then stir in the whisky.

2 Place the mixture in a loaf tin lined with cling film and freeze for 6–8 hours. Tip out of the loaf tin and remove the cling film. Cut the ice cream into slices and serve garnished with desiccated coconut.

Plum ice cream
with cinnamon

Serves 4

200 g plums
1 tbsp lemon juice
50 g sugar
¼ tsp ground cinnamon
¼ tsp ground cloves
300 ml cream
60 g vanilla sugar

Preparation time: 20 minutes
  (plus freezing time)
Per serving approx.
  308 kcal/1290 kJ
2 g P, 23 g F, 23 g CH

1 Wash the plums, slice in half, remove the stones and drizzle with the lemon juice. Add the sugar and the spices, and purée the fruit. Place the purée in the freezer to begin freezing.

2 Bring 100 ml of the cream to the boil together with the vanilla sugar, then place over a cold bain-marie and stir until cold. Stir the cream into the plum purée. Whip the rest of the cream until stiff and fold into the mixture.

3 Place in a shallow bowl and freeze for 6–7 hours, stirring through thoroughly several times.

Malaga ice cream
with dark rum

Serves 4

3 egg yolks
50 g sugar
15 g vanilla sugar
150 ml milk
200 ml cream
50 g raisins
4 cl dark rum
3 tbsp rum for soaking

Preparation time: 20 minutes
(plus cooling, infusing and
freezing time)
Per serving approx.
340 kcal/1424 kJ
5 g P, 22 g F, 25 g CH

1 Beat the egg yolks with the sugar and vanilla sugar until foamy. Combine the milk with half of the cream, heat in a saucepan until just below boiling point then stir into the egg mixture. Place the mixture over a hot bain-marie and stir until creamy, but do not allow to boil. Remove from the bain-marie, place over a bowl of ice cold water and stir until cold.

2 Whip the rest of the cream until stiff. Soak the raisins in 3 tablespoons of rum. Fold 4 cl of rum into the cold egg mixture. Place in a shallow bowl and freeze for approx. 3 hours. Carefully fold in the rum-soaked raisins and freeze the ice cream for a further 4–5 hours. Serve in scoops.

Sinfully smooth with cream and milk

Creamy ice cream
with Baileys

Serves 4

2 egg yolks

75 g sugar

200 ml cream

150 g double cream

50 g sour cream

1 tsp lemon juice

4 cl Baileys or other
  cream-based liqueur

zest from 1 untreated
  lemon for serving

Preparation time: 20 minutes
  (plus freezing time)

Per serving approx.
  408 kcal/1708 kJ

4 g P, 31 g F, 25 g CH

1 Beat the egg yolks with the sugar until foamy, add half of the cream and stir until smooth. Place in a saucepan and bring to the boil, stirring all the time. Remove from the heat, place over a cold bain-marie and stir until cold.

2 Combine the double cream with the sour cream and the lemon juice. Combine this mixture with the egg and cream mixture. Whip the rest of the cream until stiff and fold into the mixture together with the Baileys.

3 Place the mixture in a shallow bowl and freeze for approx. 7 hours, stirring through several times. Serve in scoops sprinkled with lemon zest.

Rosemary ice cream
with acacia honey

Serves 4

250 ml cream

70 g sugar

1 tbsp acacia honey

½ vanilla pod

2 sprigs of rosemary

150 g yoghurt

150 g crème fraîche

Preparation time: 20 minutes
(plus cooling and freezing
time)
Per serving approx.
390 kcal/1633 kJ
4 g P, 32 g F, 23 g CH

1 Combine the cream with the sugar, the honey, the vanilla pod and the rosemary sprigs in a saucepan and bring to the boil. Remove the saucepan from the heat and leave to cool slightly. Scrape the seeds out of the vanilla pod and discard the pod. Remove the rosemary sprigs and push the mixture through a sieve.

2 Stir the yoghurt and the crème fraîche into the cream mixture. Place the mixture in a shallow container and freeze for approx. 5 hours, stirring through thoroughly several times. Serve immediately in scoops, sprinkled with a little brittle if you like.

Creamy ice cream
with Marsala

Serves 4

4 eggs

50 g sugar

200 ml cream

1 tsp ground vanilla

½ tsp grated zest from
  1 untreated lime

½ tsp lime juice

6 cl Marsala

vanilla sauce for serving

Preparation time: 30 minutes
  (plus freezing time)

Per serving approx.
  325 kcal/1361 kJ

9 g P, 22 g F, 21 g CH

1 Separate the eggs. Beat the egg yolks with the sugar until foamy. Combine half of the cream with the ground vanilla and heat until just below boiling point. Remove from the heat and stir into the egg mixture.

2 Add the lime zest, juice and the Marsala, place over a cold bain-marie and stir until cold. Whip the rest of the cream until stiff and fold into the mixture.

3 Place the mixture in a shallow bowl and freeze for approx. 3 hours. Whisk the egg whites until soft peaks form and fold into the ice cream. Freeze for another 4 hours, stirring through thoroughly several times. Serve with vanilla sauce.

Sinfully smooth with cream and milk

Almond brittle ice cream
with bitter almond essence

Serves 4

30 g butter
2 tbsp honey
100 g chopped almonds
2 egg yolks
50 g sugar
150 ml milk
200 ml cream
2 drops bitter almond
  essence

Preparation time: 25 minutes
  (plus cooling and freezing
  time)
Per serving approx.
  465 kcal/1947 kJ
9 g P, 40 g F, 19 g CH

1 Melt the butter and stir in the honey. Add the almonds and caramelise, stirring all the time. Allow to cool, stirring all the time to prevent it sticking together.

2 Beat the egg yolks with 25 g of sugar until foamy. Combine the milk with the rest of the sugar and 100 ml of the cream and bring to the boil, stirring all the time. Stir into the beaten eggs, leave to cool and then place in a shallow container. Chill for approx. 1 hour.

3 Whip the rest of the cream until stiff and add to the ice cream mixture together with the bitter almond essence. Freeze for approx. 2 hours and then fold in $2/3$ of the almond brittle. Freeze for another 4–5 hours, stirring through thoroughly several times. Serve sprinkled with the rest of the almond brittle.

Creamy chocolate cookie
ice cream

Serves 6

3 eggs

300 ml whipping cream

50 g icing sugar

50 g chocolate cookies

Preparation time: 30 minutes
 (plus freezing time)

Per serving approx.

 243 kcal/1017 kJ

6 g P, 20 g F, 12 g CH

1 Separate the eggs. Whisk the egg whites until stiff and, separately, whip the cream until stiff. Beat the egg yolks with the sugar until foamy. Carefully fold the egg whites and the cream into the egg mixture. Place the mixture in a shallow dish and freeze for approx. 2 hours, stirring through every 30 minutes.

2 Crush the chocolate cookies in a plastic bag and fold into the ice cream mixture after 2 hours. Freeze for another 2 hours, stirring through several times. Serve in dessert bowls.

Chocolate ice cream
with chilli powder

Serves 4

6 tbsp cocoa powder
100 ml milk
250 ml cream
5 tbsp acacia honey
½ tsp chilli powder

Preparation time: 15 minutes
(plus cooling and freezing
time)
Per serving approx.
265 kcal/1110 kJ
4 g P, 21 g F, 14 g CH

1 Combine the cocoa and the milk and heat, stirring all the time, but do not boil. Whizz in a blender and leave to cool.

2 Whip the cream until stiff and fold into the cocoa milk together with the honey. Leave to cool. Stir in the chilli powder. Place the mixture in a shallow bowl and freeze for 5–6 hours.

Marzipan ice cream
with amaretto and rosewater

Serves 4

100 g raw marzipan
200 ml milk
25 g sugar
2 tsp amaretto
1 tsp rosewater
200 ml cream
waffles and chocolate
  sauce to serve

Preparation time: 15 minutes
  (plus cooling and freezing
  time)
Per serving approx.
  323 kcal/1352 kJ
4 g P, 21 g F, 27 g CH

1 Crumble the marzipan, combine with the milk and the sugar and heat, stirring all the time, but do not boil. Blend the marzipan milk in a blender until smooth. Add the amaretto and rosewater, and leave to cool.

2 Whip the cream until stiff and fold into the mixture. Place the mixture in a shallow bowl and freeze for 5–6 hours, stirring through several times. Serve with waffles and chocolate sauce.

TIP

You can also make the marzipan yourself: for approx. 200 g of marzipan, skin 100 g of almonds and grind them very finely. Combine with 100 g of icing sugar, 1 drop of bitter almond essence and 1–2 tbsp of rosewater and stir until smooth.

Sinfully smooth with cream and milk   175

Ice cream stars
with coconut and peanut brittle

Makes 12

1 tbsp desiccated coconut
6 egg yolks + 4 eggs
150 g sugar
1 l cream
2 cl coconut liqueur
2 heaped tsp cinnamon
4 cl cinnamon liqueur
  (or rum)
50 g peanut brittle
frozen raspberries and
  gooseberries to serve

Preparation time: 50 minutes
  (plus cooling and freezing
  time)
Per serving approx.
  351 kcal/1474 kJ
  6 g P, 28 g F, 14 g CH

1 Dry fry the desiccated coconut in a frying pan. Beat the egg yolks with the eggs and the sugar over a hot bain-marie until foamy. Place over a cold bain-marie and beat until cold. Whip the cream until stiff and fold in. Remove ⅓ of the mixture and combine with the coconut liqueur, then chill.

2 Carefully combine the rest of the mixture with the ground cinnamon and the cinnamon liqueur (or rum). Line a baking tin with baking paper. Spread the cinnamon mixture over the base and freeze for 30 minutes.

3 Combine the desiccated coconut and the peanut brittle. Spread the coconut cream over the cinnamon ice cream, sprinkle with the coconut brittle and freeze overnight. Cut star shapes out of the ice cream and arrange on plates, garnished with raspberries and gooseberries, and serve immediately.

Pistachio ice cream
classic, and so good

Serves 4

120 g pistachio nuts
1 vanilla pod
500 ml cream
200 g sugar
5 egg yolks

Preparation time: 25 minutes
  (plus cooling and freezing
  time)
Per serving approx.
  850 kcal/3550 kJ
  11 g P, 65 g F, 57 g CH

1 Finely grind the pistachio nuts in a blender. Slice open the vanilla pod with a sharp knife, scrape out the seeds and place the pod together with the seeds in a saucepan and 250 ml of the cream. Add 100 g of the sugar and heat, stirring all the time. Switch off the heat and leave to cool slowly. Remove the vanilla pod.

2 Beat the egg yolks with the rest of the sugar until pale yellow and foamy. In a second bowl, whip the cream until stiff. Stir the ground pistachio nuts into the liquid cream, then stir in the egg yolk mixture and combine with the whipped cream.

3 Place the ice cream mixture in a suitable container (ideally stainless steel) and freeze for approx. 5 hours in a freezer or ice cream maker.

Sinfully smooth with cream and milk

Banana ice cream
classic, and so good

Serves 4

3 bananas
1 tbsp lemon juice
300 ml cream
2 egg yolks
60 g sugar
30 g vanilla sugar

Preparation time: 25 minutes
  (plus freezing time)
Per serving approx.
  400 kcal/1670 kJ
5 g P, 26 g F, 38 g CH

1 Peel and slice the bananas (you will need approx. 275 g sliced banana). Place in a deep bowl together with the lemon juice and 150 ml of the cream, and blend with a hand blender until smooth.

2 Whip the rest of the cream in a second bowl until stiff. In a third bowl, whisk the egg yolks with the sugar and vanilla sugar until pale yellow and creamy.

3 Combine the banana purée with the egg yolk cream and fold in the whipped cream. Either freeze in an ice cream maker or place in a suitable bowl (ideally stainless steel) and leave in the freezer for approx. 5 hours.

Sinfully smooth with cream and milk

Strawberry ice cream
classic, and so good

Serves 4

500 g strawberries

2 tbsp lemon juice

150 g sugar

4 egg yolks

400 ml cream

Preparation time: 25 minutes
(plus freezing time)

Per serving approx.
560 kcal/2340 kJ
7 g P, 38 g F, 49 g CH

1 Wash the strawberries and pat dry. Place in a bowl with the lemon juice and half of the sugar, and purée.

2 Place the rest of the sugar in a second bowl together with the egg yolks and beat until pale yellow and creamy.

3 Whip the cream in a third bowl until stiff. Combine the strawberry purée with the egg yolk mixture and then fold in the whipped cream. Either freeze in an ice cream maker or place in the freezer for approx. 5 hours, ideally in a pre-chilled metal container.

Sinfully smooth with cream and milk

Smurf ice cream
easy and different

Serves 4

250 g Greek yoghurt,
  natural (10 % FDM)
100 g icing sugar
2 tsp lemon juice
250 ml cream
a few drops of blue food
  colouring

Preparation time: 15 minutes
  (plus freezing time)
Per serving approx.
  360 kcal/1500 kJ
4 g P, 25 g F, 29 g CH

1 Mix together the yoghurt with the icing sugar and the lemon juice until smooth. Whip the cream until stiff and fold in. Stir in as much blue food colouring as is required to reach the shade you want.

2 Either freeze the ice cream mixture in an ice cream maker or place in a suitable container (ideally stainless steel) and leave in the freezer for approx. 5 hours.

TIP

You can also make this ice cream using blue (Smurf) ice cream powder available from a variety of online shops on the internet.

Melt-in-your-mouth
parfaits

Cherry parfait
laced with schnapps

Serves 4

100 g tinned sour
  cherries, stoned
50 ml cherry schnapps
1 vanilla pod
250 ml milk
250 ml whipping cream
5 egg yolks
75 g sugar
lemon balm for
  garnishing

Preparation time: 30 minutes
  (plus infusing, cooling and
  freezing time)
Per serving approx.
  493 kcal/2064 kJ
  10 g P, 33 g F, 31 g CH

1 Drain the cherries, retaining 50 ml of the juice. Purée 50 g of the cherries with the juice and the cherry schnapps.

2 Cut the vanilla pod in half lengthways and scrape out the seeds. Place the milk and half of the cream in a saucepan together with the vanilla pod and the vanilla seeds. Bring to the boil and leave to infuse for 30 minutes. Remove the vanilla pod and heat the mixture again.

3 Beat the egg yolks with the sugar until foamy, add to the cream and milk mixture, stirring all the time, but do not allow to boil. Place over a cold bain-marie and stir until cold. Add the cherry purée. Whip the rest of the cream until stiff and fold in. Transfer the mixture to a mould and freeze for approx. 7 hours. Serve garnished with lemon balm leaves and the remaining cherries.

Caramel nut parfait
with rum

Serves 4

2 eggs
4 egg yolks
130 g sugar
70 g chopped walnuts
50 g nut nougat
2 tsp rum
350 ml cream

Preparation time: 30 minutes
 (plus freezing time)
Per serving approx.
 687 kcal/2876 kJ
13 g P, 50 g F, 46 g CH

1 Beat the eggs with the egg yolks and 100 g of the sugar until foamy then stir over a hot bain-marie until creamy. Place over a cold bain-marie and stir until cold. Add the rest of the sugar to 2 tablespoons of water in a frying pan and caramelise, stirring all the time. Add the chopped walnuts.

2 Melt the nut nougat, stirring all the time, combine with the rum and stir into the egg mixture. Mix in the nuts and leave to cool. Whip the cream until stiff and fold in. Place the mixture in the freezer for approx. 5 hours. Thaw the parfait slightly before serving.

Melt-in-your-mouth parfaits

Cinnamon parfait
with rum

Serves 6

4 eggs

100 g acacia honey

50 ml milk

1 ¼ tbsp ground cinnamon

350 ml cream

rum

25 g sugar

Preparation time: 20 minutes
  (plus freezing time)
Per serving approx.
  460 kcal/1926 kJ
10 g P, 34 g F, 29 g CH

1 Separate the eggs. Combine the egg yolks with the honey and the milk, and beat over a hot bain-marie until creamy. Place over a cold bain-marie and stir until cold. Sprinkle the cinnamon over, stir in the rum. Whip the cream until stiff and fold in. Whisk the egg whites with the sugar until stiff and fold into the cream mixture.

2 Transfer the mixture into a shallow bowl and freeze for approx. 5 hours, stirring several times. Serve garnished with cream rosettes and grated chocolate as desired.

Caramel coffee parfait
with peanut pieces

Serves 4

185 g icing sugar

150 ml milk

3 egg yolks

½ tbsp instant coffee

300 ml cream

60 g chocolate-covered
  peanuts

Preparation time: 30 minutes
  (plus cooling and freezing
  time)
Per serving approx.
  483 kcal/2022 kJ
10 g P, 36 g F, 31 g CH

1 Combine 120 g of the icing sugar with 40 ml of water in a saucepan, stir until the sugar has dissolved and bring to the boil. Simmer for 4 minutes until it forms a pale caramel then remove from the heat and allow to cool slightly.

2 Add the milk, return to the heat and stir until the caramel dissolves, stirring all the time. Beat the egg yolks with the rest of the icing sugar until foamy, dissolve the coffee powder in 1 tablespoon of water. Add the milk mixture and the coffee to the beaten eggs, place over a hot bain-marie and stir until creamy. Place over an ice cold bain-marie and stir until cold.

3 Whip the cream until stiff and fold in. Place the mixture in a shallow container and freeze for 2 hours. Chop the peanuts and fold into the ice cream. Freeze for a further 2–3 hours.

Espresso parfait
with orange liqueur

Serves 4
6 egg yolks
200 g sugar
400 ml cold espresso
1 cl orange liqueur
250 ml cream

Preparation time: 15 minutes
  (plus freezing time)
Per serving approx.
  490 kcal/2050 kJ
6 g P, 28 g F, 52 g CH

1 Beat the egg yolks and the sugar until thick, pale and creamy. Stir in the espresso and then the orange liqueur.

2 Whip the cream until stiff and carefully fold into the espresso mixture. Rinse out a parfait mould with cold water and line with cling film. Pour the mixture into the mould and freeze for several hours, ideally overnight.

3 Tip the parfait out of the mould, remove the cling film and cut into slices. Serve immediately.

TIP

For the orange liqueur you can use Cointreau, for example, a liqueur made from orange peel and with an alcohol content of 40%, or Grand Marnier.

Mulled wine parfait
with cardamom

Serves 4

1 vanilla pod

1 organic orange

3 cardamom pods

500 ml dry red wine
 (e.g. Merlot)

1 cinnamon stick

4 cloves

4 egg yolks

200 g sieved icing sugar

400 ml cream

8 dates

1 tsp cinnamon sugar
 according to taste

Preparation time: 25 minutes
 (plus cooking and freezing
 time)
Per serving approx.
 604 kcal/2537 kJ
 4 g P, 32 g F, 56 g CH

1 Slice the vanilla pod in half lengthways and scrape out the seeds. Wash the orange, rub dry, finely grate the zest and cut the flesh into segments. Open the cardamom pods and remove the black seeds. Place the red wine in a saucepan together with the spices and the orange zest, bring to the boil and simmer for a while.

2 Beat the egg yolks with the icing sugar over a bain-marie until pale and foamy, then remove from the bain-marie. Strain the mulled wine, put one quarter aside and gradually add the rest to the egg mixture. Beat the mixture until it is cold, light and foamy. Whip the cream until stiff and fold in.

3 Divide the mixture into portions and freeze for approx. 12 hours. Stone the dates, slice them open so that they fan out and place them, together with the orange segments, in the rest of the cooled mulled wine. Serve the parfait sprinkled with cinnamon sugar according to taste and arranged with the orange segments and the dates on the plates, drizzled with the rest of the mulled wine.

Nougat parfait
with flaked almonds

Serves 6

100 g flaked almonds

4 eggs

3 tbsp sugar

3 tbsp honey

100 g nut nougat (firm
  enough for cutting)

250 ml cream

Preparation time: 30 minutes
  (plus freezing time)
Per serving approx.
  440 kcal/1848 kJ
11 g P, 31 g F, 26 g CH

1 Dry fry the almonds in a frying pan. Separate the eggs. Beat the egg yolks, sugar and honey over a hot bain-marie for 5–6 minutes until creamy. Dice the nougat and melt over a hot bain-marie. Fold the warm, liquid nougat into the egg mixture and leave to cool slightly.

2 Line a loaf tin (approx. 1 l in volume) or an empty ice cream carton with cling film. Whisk the egg whites until stiff and, separately, whip the cream until stiff. Set aside 1 tablespoon of the almonds and fold the rest into the egg mixture, then fold in the cream and lastly the whisked egg whites. Place the parfait mixture in the mould, cover and freeze for at least 6 hours, ideally overnight.

3 Tip the parfait out of the mould and then either slice it or use an ice cream scoop to serve. Sprinkle with the rest of the almonds.

Vanilla parfait
with crumbed biscuits

Serves 4

100 g sponge fingers
2 eggs
2 egg yolks
120 g sugar
pinch of salt
1 vanilla pod
30 g vanilla sugar
400 ml cream

Preparation time: 25 minutes
 (plus freezing time)
Per serving approx.
 630 kcal/2630 kJ
10 g P, 39 g F, 58 g CH

1 Crush the sponge fingers with a rolling pin. Separate the eggs. Beat all 4 egg yolks with the sugar until pale yellow and foamy. Whisk the egg whites with a pinch of salt in a second clean bowl until stiff.

2 Slice open the vanilla pod, scrape out the seeds. Place in a third bowl together with the vanilla sugar and the cream, and beat until stiff.

3 Carefully combine all 3 of the beaten mixtures using a wooden spoon and fold in the crushed sponge biscuits. Place in a suitable loaf tin and freeze for approx. 6 hours.

4 Shortly before serving, briefly dip the loaf tin in hot water up to the rim then tip out the parfait. Alternatively, thaw the parfait slightly and then tip out. Slice the parfait and serve on a bed of fruit purée of your taste.

Poppy seed parfait
simply delicious

Serves 4

100 g poppy seeds
1 vanilla pod
180 ml milk
130 g sugar
4 egg yolks
300 ml cream

Preparation time: 25 minutes
   (plus cooking, cooling and
   freezing time)
Per serving approx.
   570 kcal/2380 kJ
12 g P, 42 g F, 38 g CH

1 Grind the poppy seeds with a hand blender or in old electric coffee grinder. Slice open the vanilla pod and scrape out the seeds. Place the milk with 50 g of the sugar in a saucepan and heat. Add the poppy seeds, vanilla seeds and the vanilla pod and simmer for approx. 10 minutes, stirring all the time. Remove the pod and take the saucepan off the heat.

2 Beat the egg yolks with the rest of the sugar until pale yellow and foamy. Gradually stir in the still warm poppy seed mixture and allow to chill completely in the fridge.

3 Whip the cream until stiff, fold into the cold poppy seed mixture and pour into 4 suitable moulds or cups. Cover with cling film and freeze for approx. 5 hours. Thaw slightly before serving and tip out of the moulds or cups.

Pumpkin seed parfait
with pumpkin seed oil

Serves 4

100 g pumpkin seeds
180 g sugar
4 egg yolks
1 tbsp pumpkin seed oil
450 ml cream

Preparation time: 25 minutes
  (plus browning, hardening
  and freezing time)
Per serving approx.
  750 kcal/3130 kJ
12 g P, 55 g F, 52 g CH

1 Dry fry the pumpkin seeds in a frying pan to brown them, stirring all the time, for approx. 10 minutes and then take them out. Put half of the sugar in the frying pan and melt to form a golden caramel, stirring all the time. Combine the pumpkin seeds with the melted sugar and immediately place on a sheet of baking paper. Smooth over, then allow to cool and harden. Grind in a blender.

2 Beat the egg yolks with the rest of the sugar until pale yellow and foamy, then stir in the pumpkin seed oil and the ground pumpkin seeds.

3 Whip the cream until stiff and fold in. Place in a suitable loaf tin or parfait mould, cover with cling film and freeze for approx. 6 hours. Thaw slightly before serving and tip out of the mould.

White chocolate parfait
simply delicious

Serves 4

400 ml cream

125 g sugar

5 egg yolks

125 g white couverture
chocolate

1 cl cherry schnapps
according to taste

Preparation time: 25 minutes
(plus cooling and freezing
time)

Per serving approx.
640 kcal/2670 kJ
10 g P, 42 g F, 54 g CH

1 Whip the cream until stiff and place in the fridge until required. Place the sugar in a saucepan with 30 ml of water, bring to the boil and simmer until syrupy, then remove from the heat. Beat the egg yolks in a bowl and then gradually whisk into the hot sugar syrup until pale yellow and foamy.

2 Break the white couverture chocolate into pieces and melt over a bain-marie. Fold the melted chocolate into the egg yolk mixture, flavour with cherry schnapps according to taste and then stir until cold.

3 Fold in the whipped cream and then place the mixture in a suitable loaf tin or parfait mould and freeze for approx. 5 hours. Thaw slightly before serving and tip out of the mould.

Hazelnut parfait
with nut liqueur

Serves 4

200 g sugar
150 g chopped hazelnuts
2 eggs
4 egg yolks
pinch of salt
450 ml cream
50 g forest honey
2 tbsp nut liqueur

Preparation time: 30 minutes
  (plus hardening and freezing
  time)
Per serving approx.
  950 kcal/3970 kJ
15 g P, 68 g F, 69 g CH

1 Caramelise 150 g of the sugar in a frying pan until pale brown. Then remove the frying pan from the heat and stir in the hazelnuts. Pour the hazelnut brittle onto a sheet of baking paper, smooth over and leave to cool and harden. Finely grind in a blender.

2 Separate the eggs. Beat all of the egg yolks with the rest of the sugar until pale yellow and creamy. Stir in the ground hazelnuts. With clean whisks, beat the egg whites with a pinch of salt until stiff. In a third bowl, whip the cream until stiff and fold in the honey.

3 Combine the 3 beaten mixtures and then flavour with the nut liqueur. Pour into a suitable parfait mould or loaf tin and freeze for approx. 5 hours. Thaw slightly, tip out of the mould and serve.

Gelateria

Pineapple yoghurt ice cream
with fruit

Serves 4

For the yoghurt ice cream:

200 g Greek yoghurt
(10% FDM)
1 tbsp lemon juice
100 g icing sugar
180 g fresh pineapple
350 ml cream
60 g vanilla sugar

Also:

200 ml cream
fruit pieces of your choice
for garnishing

Preparation time: 15 minutes
(plus freezing time)
Per serving approx.
630 kcal/2360 kJ
5 g P, 46 g F, 48 g CH

1 Combine the yoghurt with the lemon juice and icing sugar, and stir until smooth. Remove the peel, the core and the eyes from the pineapple. Purée with a hand blender (you will need approx. 150 g pineapple purée). Whip the cream with the vanilla sugar until stiff.

2 Combine the yoghurt with the stiff, whipped cream. Pour ⅔ of the mixture into a suitable bowl (ideally stainless steel), cover with cling film and freeze for approx. 6 hours. Combine the last third of the yoghurt mixture with the pineapple purée, pour into a bowl, cover and also freeze for approx. 6 hours, using a hand blender to stir after approx. 1 hour.

3 To serve, whip the cream until stiff. Scoop out portions from both types of ice cream and arrange decoratively in glasses with fresh fruit and whipped cream.

Caramel ice cream
with walnut brittle

Serves 4

For the caramel ice cream:
170 g sugar
200 ml cream
350 ml milk
2 eggs
pinch of salt
2 egg yolks

For the brittle:
100 g sugar
100 g walnuts, roughly
  chopped

Also:
200 ml cream
nut liqueur

Preparation time: 70 minutes
  (plus freezing time)
Per serving approx.
  880 kcal/3670 kJ
15 g P, 56 g F, 79 g CH

1 For the caramel ice cream, caramelise 100 g of sugar in a frying pan until light brown. Pour in the cream and the milk, and simmer until the caramel has completely dissolved, stirring all the time.

2 Separate the eggs. Whisk the egg whites with a pinch of salt until stiff and place in the fridge until required. Beat the egg yolks with the rest of the sugar over a hot bain-marie until pale yellow and foamy. Gradually pour in the hot caramel milk, stirring until the mixture thickens. Remove from the bain-marie, place over an ice cold bain-marie and stir until cold. Fold in the beaten egg whites and freeze in an ice cream maker or in the freezer for approx. 6 hours.

3 For the brittle, caramelise the sugar in a non-stick frying pan until light brown. Stir in the chopped walnuts and immediately spread the mixture over a sheet of baking paper, smooth over and leave to cool. Then chop into pieces.

4 To serve, whip the cream until stiff. Serve the caramel ice cream in scoops, 3 per serving, garnished with whipped cream, walnut brittle and nut liqueur.

Banana split
with chocolate ice cream

Serves 4
For the chocolate
ice cream:

75 g dark chocolate
75 g milk chocolate
175 ml milk
100 g sugar
400 ml cream

Also:

200 ml cream
2 bananas
chocolate sauce

Preparation time: 40 minutes
   (plus freezing time)
Per serving approx.
   830 kcal/3460 kJ
10 g P, 55 g F, 73 g CH

1 Chop the chocolate and melt over a bain-marie. Add the milk and the sugar, and stir until thick and smooth. Remove from the bain-marie and stir until cold.

2 Whip the cream until stiff and fold into the chocolate mixture. Either freeze in an ice cream maker or pour into a suitable bowl (ideally stainless steel) and freeze in the freezer for approx. 6 hours, stirring with a hand blender after 1 hour of freezing time.

3 Whip the cream until stiff. Peel the bananas and cut in half lengthways. Arrange on elongated plates together with scoops of the chocolate ice cream. Decorate generously with whipped cream and chocolate sauce, and serve.

Spaghetti ice cream
a classic

Serves 4
For the vanilla ice cream:
1 vanilla pod
250 ml milk
80 g sugar
3 egg yolks
250 g crème fraîche

For the strawberry sauce:
250 g strawberries
1 tsp lemon juice
60 g vanilla sugar

Also:
200 ml cream
grated white chocolate
   for garnishing

Preparation time: 45 minutes
   (plus cooling and freezing
   time)
Per serving approx.
   600 kcal/2500 kJ
8 g P, 47 g F, 35 g CH

1 Slice open the vanilla pod with a sharp knife and scrape out the seeds. Pour the milk into a saucepan with half of the sugar, add the vanilla pod and seeds and bring to the boil, stirring all the time. Remove the vanilla pod.

2 Beat the egg yolks with the rest of the sugar over a hot bain-marie until pale yellow and foamy. Gradually stir in the hot vanilla milk and keep stirring until the mixture thickens. Remove from the bain-marie and strain through a fine sieve.

3 Stir in the crème fraîche then place the mixture over an ice cold bain-marie and stir until cold. Pour into a suitable bowl (ideally stainless steel), cover with cling film and freeze for approx. 4 hours in the freezer or use an ice cream maker.

4 If the vanilla ice cream is frozen too solid, thaw slightly before serving. In the meantime, wash the strawberries, pat dry and then purée together with the lemon juice and vanilla sugar. Whip the cream until very stiff and divide among 4 dessert plates.

5 Push portions of the vanilla ice cream through a potato press directly onto the cream. Pour over the strawberry sauce and serve garnished with grated white chocolate.

Amarena cherry ice cream
in a glass cup

Serves 4

For the Amarena cherry ice cream:

250 ml cream
100 g natural yoghurt
100 g crème fraîche
60 g vanilla sugar
200 g Amarena cherries
  (tinned)

Also:

200 ml cream
Amarena cherries and
  syrup (tinned)

Preparation time: 10 minutes
  (plus freezing time)
Per serving approx.
  510 kcal/2130 kJ
5 g P, 45 g F, 22 g CH

1 Whip the cream until stiff. Combine the natural yoghurt with the crème fraîche and stir until smooth. Stir in the vanilla sugar and the Amarena cherries. Fold in the stiffly whipped cream.

2 Either freeze the mixture in an ice cream maker or pour into a container (ideally stainless steel) and place in the freezer for approx. 6 hours, stirring several times with a fork.

3 To serve, whip the cream until stiff. Start with a little whipped cream in each serving glass, followed by some Amarena cherries and syrup, and then 3 scoops per glass of ice cream on top. Garnish with the remaining cream, Amarena cherries and syrup.

Neapolitan ice cream
gateau

Serves 4

150 g sponge fingers
50 g florentines
250 g strawberries
340 g sugar
juice and grated zest from
 ½ an untreated lemon
200 g dark chocolate
 (70% cocoa)
3 eggs
6 egg yolks
850 ml cream
seeds from 1 vanilla pod
strawberries for
 garnishing

Preparation time: 90 minutes
 (plus freezing time)
Per serving approx.
 540 kcal/2260 kJ
8 g P, 32 g F, 54 g CH

1 Line the rim of a spring form tin or a cake ring with baking paper and place on a baking tray lined with baking paper. Line the base with the sponge fingers, closely packed.

2 Finely chop the florentines. Wash the strawberries, drain well and then purée. Add 120 g of the sugar as well as the lemon juice and zest to the purée and stir well. Melt the chocolate over a hot bain-marie and leave to cool slightly.

3 In another bowl beat the eggs and egg yolks with 200 g sugar over a hot bain-marie until warm. Then place over a cold bain-marie and stir until cold. Whip 600 ml of the cream until stiff and fold into the egg mixture. Combine one third of the mixture with the liquid chocolate, add the chopped florentines and stir until smooth. Spread the mixture over the sponge biscuits and smooth the surface.

4 Combine the second third of the egg mixture with the strawberry purée, carefully spread over the chocolate mixture and smooth the surface.

5 Stir the vanilla seeds into the remaining egg mixture and spread over the strawberry layer. Freeze the gateau overnight. Whip the rest of the cream with 20 g of sugar until stiff. Decorate the gateau with the cream and fresh strawberries.

Macchiato
with Baileys ice cream

Serves 4

200 ml fat-free milk

100 ml coffee cream

45 ml Baileys

2 tbsp cocoa powder,
  unsweetened

50 ml cream

1 egg white

1 tbsp icing sugar

pinch of salt

200 ml espresso

cinnamon for dusting

Preparation time: 30 minutes
  (plus cooling and freezing
  time)
Per serving approx.
  169 kcal/708 kJ
4 g P, 11 g F, 11 g CH

1 Place 100 ml of the milk in a saucepan together with the coffee cream, 35 ml of Baileys and the cocoa powder, and bring to the boil, stirring all the time. Remove from the heat, stir in the sugar and leave until cold. Whip the cream until stiff, fold into the Baileys milk and chill for approx. 1 hour.

2 Whisk the egg white with the icing sugar and salt until stiff and then stir into the milk mixture. Pour into a bowl and freeze for approx. 6 hours, stirring through thoroughly several times. Fold in the rest of the Baileys a couple of hours before the end of the freezing time.

3 Heat the rest of the milk and whisk until frothy. Divide the freshly brewed espresso between 4 cups and pour in the milk foam. Place 1 scoop of Baileys ice cream in each cup and dust with cinnamon.

Iced coffee
with vanilla ice cream

Serves 4
For the vanilla ice cream:
1 vanilla pod
125 ml milk
250 ml cream
3 egg yolks
50 g sugar

Also:
100 ml cream
800 ml strong coffee, ice cold
sugar
chocolate sprinkles for garnishing

Preparation time: 40 minutes (plus freezing time)
Per serving approx.
380 kcal/1580 kJ
6 g P, 33 g F, 17 g CH

1 For the vanilla ice cream, slice open the vanilla pod with a sharp knife and scrape out the seeds. Place in a saucepan with the milk and half of the cream and bring to the boil, stirring all the time. Remove the pod.

2 Beat the egg yolks with the sugar over a hot bain-marie until pale yellow and creamy, then gradually pour in the hot vanilla milk, stirring all the time until the mixture thickens. Remove from the heat, place over an ice cold bain-marie and stir until cold.

3 Whip the rest of the cream until stiff and fold in. Freeze in an ice cream maker or pour into a suitable container (ideally stainless steel) and freeze in the freezer for approx. 6 hours, stirring through thoroughly several times with a fork.

4 To serve, whip the cream until stiff. Place scoops of the vanilla ice cream in 4 tall glasses. Sweeten the ice cold coffee with sugar according to taste and pour over the vanilla ice cream. Garnish each glass with a dollop of whipped cream and chocolate sprinkles.

Milkshake
with mango ice cream

Serves 4

For the ice cream:

1 ripe mango

½ lime

50 g sugar

30 g vanilla sugar

100 g crème fraîche

150 ml cream

For the milkshake:

1 ripe mango

½ lime

1 tbsp sugar

300 ml milk

Preparation time: 30 minutes
  (plus freezing time)
Per serving approx.
  400 kcal/1670 kJ
5 g P, 24 g F, 39 g CH

1 Wash and peel the mango, remove the flesh from the stone and cut into pieces. Squeeze the juice from the lime. Purée the mango with the lime juice and the sugar.

2 Stir the vanilla sugar into the crème fraîche and combine with the mango purée. Whip the cream until stiff and fold in. Freeze the mixture in an ice cream maker or pour into a suitable container (ideally stainless steel) and freeze in the freezer for approx. 4 hours, stirring through several times with a fork.

3 For the milkshake, wash and peel the mango, remove the flesh from the stone and cut into pieces. Set aside a number of pieces for the garnish and place the rest in the freezer for approx. 20 minutes. Squeeze the juice from the lime. Purée the semi-frozen mango pieces with the lime juice and the sugar. Add the cold milk and the ice cream. Purée until foamy and divide between the glasses. Garnish with the mango pieces you set aside.

Tartufo
with truffle and vanilla ice cream

Serves 6

For the vanilla ice cream:

1 vanilla pod

250 ml milk

80 g sugar

3 egg yolks

250 g crème fraîche

For the truffle ice cream:

400 ml cream

150 g dark chocolate

2 tbsp sugar

4 tbsp cherry schnapps

Also:

cocoa powder for dusting

200 ml cream for
  garnishing

chocolate sauce for
  garnishing

Amarena cherries for
  garnishing

Preparation time: 60 minutes
(plus chilling, freezing and
softening time)
Per serving approx.
720 kcal/3000 kJ
8 g P, 60 g F, 34 g CH

1 Slice open the vanilla pod and scrape out the seeds. Bring the milk together with half of the sugar, the vanilla pod and the seeds to the boil, stirring all the time. Remove the vanilla pod. Beat the egg yolks with the rest of the sugar over a hot bain-marie until pale yellow and foamy. Gradually stir in the hot vanilla milk and keep stirring until the mixture thickens. Remove from the bain-marie and strain through a fine sieve. Stir in the crème fraîche, place over an ice cold bain-marie and stir until cold. Freeze the mixture for approx. 4 hours or use an ice cream maker.

2 For the truffle ice cream, heat the cream in a saucepan. Chop the chocolate and add to the milk together with the sugar. Keep stirring the cream until the chocolate has melted and then stir in the cherry schnapps. Leave to cool completely, then chill in the fridge for at least 4 hours and beat again with a hand mixer. Then freeze the mixture for approx. 4 hours.

3 For the tartufo, thaw both types of ice cream slightly. Dust 6 dessert plates with cocoa powder. Whip the cream until stiff and place in the centre of the plates. Roll a very small ball of truffle ice cream to start with, then coat this with vanilla ice cream and finally with a further thin layer of truffle ice cream. Roll in cocoa powder and place 1 tartufo on the whipped cream on each plate. Serve garnished with chocolate sauce and Amarena cherries.

Mint ice cream
with chocolate chunks

Makes 16

200 ml cream

2 egg yolks

1 tsp icing sugar

pinch of salt

50 ml peppermint syrup

16 chilled mint chocolate
wafers

100 g dark couverture
chocolate (70 % cocoa)

Preparation time: 25 minutes
(plus cooling and freezing
time)

Per piece approx.
110 kcal/460 kJ
2 g P, 6 g F, 12 g CH

1 Heat the cream in a saucepan. In another saucepan, beat the egg yolks with the icing sugar and salt until pale, thick and creamy, then gradually stir in the peppermint syrup. Pour in the hot cream. Gently heat the mixture, stirring all the time until it starts to thicken. Leave to cool for approx. 30 minutes – stirring through now and again – and then place in the fridge for 30 minutes.

2 Chop the chocolate wafers into small pieces. Stir the ice cream mixture through again then fold in the chocolate wafer pieces. Freeze, stirring through thoroughly now and again.

3 Chill a plastic chopping board in the freezer. Temper the couverture chocolate. Using an ice cream scoop, make 16 scoops, dip in the couverture chocolate and place on the chilled board: the chocolate will harden immediately. Either serve immediately or keep in the freezer.

Ice cream chocolates
small and sophisticated

Makes approx. 30

300 ml ice cream (flavour
  of your choice)
100 g couverture
  chocolate (e.g. white for
  chocolate and fruit ice
  cream, dark for vanilla
  ice cream)

Preparation time: 25 minutes
  (plus freezing time)
Per piece approx.
  220 kcal/920 kJ
4 g P, 5 g F, 35 g CH

1 Chill several plates in the freezer for 3–4 hours. Use an ice cream scoop to place 30 scoops of ice cream (approx. 30 mm in diameter) on the plates and return to the freezer.

2 Temper the couverture chocolate. Take the ice cream scoops out of the freezer in portions, dip in the couverture, allow the excess to drip off and then freeze through, covered, in the freezer for approx. 1 day.

Index

Espresso parfait with orange liqueur	197	Lychee ice cream with glacé ginger*	132
Espresso ricotta ice cream with Sambuca*	117	Macchiato with Baileys ice cream*	227
Fruits of the forest sorbet with orange and pear juice*	85	Malaga ice cream with dark rum*	160
Grape sorbet with figs*	80	Mango sorbet with lime*	67
Grapefruit granita	25	Marzipan ice cream with amaretto and rosewater*	175
Green tea sorbet with limoncello*	45	Melon granita with mint	12
Hazelnut ice cream with hazelnut liqueur*	149	Melon sorbet with honeydew melon*	62
Hazelnut parfait with nut liqueur*	210	Melon sorbet with sparkling wine*	73
Hibiscus flower granita with honey	22	Milkshake with mango ice cream	231
Honey ice cream with double cream *	102	Mint ice cream with chocolate chunks	235
Ice cream chocolates	236	Mint ice cream with sour milk*	145
Ice cream pudding with glacé fruit	129	Mint sorbet*	59
Ice cream stars with coconut and peanut brittle	177	Mulled wine parfait with cardamom	198
Iced coffee with vanilla ice cream*	229	Neapolitan ice cream gateau	224
Kiwi fruit ice cream with buttermilk*	88	Nougat parfait with flaked almonds	201
Lemon cream ice cream with buttermilk*	115	Orange ice cream with Cointreau*	134
Lemongrass ice cream with maple syrup*	125	Orange sorbet with Campari*	36
Lemon sorbet with basil	53	Papaya quark ice cream with ginger*	110
Lime ice cream with yoghurt and quark*	108	Papaya sorbet*	41
		Passion fruit ice cream with yoghurt*	98
		Passion fruit sorbet*	82

* Can also be made using an ice cream maker.